taking the **OLD TESTAMENT CHALLENGE**

JUDSON POLING

ZONDERVAN™
GRAND RAPIDS, MICHIGAN 49530 USA

WILLOW
Willow Creek Resources

We want to hear from you. Please send your comments about this book to us in care of zreview@zondervan.com. Thank you.

ZONDERVAN™

Taking the Old Testament Challenge
Copyright © 2003 by Willow Creek Association

Requests for information should be addressed to:
Zondervan, *Grand Rapids, Michigan 49530*

ISBN 0-310-24913-9

Interior design by Sharon VanLoozenoord
Interior production by Beth Shagene
Printed in the United States of America

05 06 07 08 09 /❖ DC/ 10 9

C⊙NTENTS

introduction

Imagine you're in heaven and the prophet Zechariah walks up to you and asks, "So, what did you think of my book?"

You sheepishly look down, shuffle your feet, and mutter, "Uh, I never read it."

You're going to be in good company. Few people have read Zechariah's prophecy—much less the whole Old Testament. (Zechariah is right after Haggai, in case you're wondering.)

In one sense, it's easy to understand why. We're a TV-watching, Internet-wired generation. Today messages and communications come at us at a rapid-fire pace that would have left poor Zechariah reeling. We select text and click "delete" on more information in one week than most of the biblical writers had access to in a lifetime. Are we really expected to slog through the entire Old Testament with its "begats," genealogies, and repetition? Who's got the time? Show us the "Executive Summary," or maybe we'll scan the "FAQs." But read every word? We've got a whole screen full of emails to answer!

What if there's something in those pages we shouldn't miss? What if hidden among those lists of names and hard-to-pronounce places is truth that would change our lives? Just suppose we committed to regular breaks in our week when we would turn off the TV, power down the computer, and spend some time reading this classic. Imagine what might happen in our lives.

It's true: The Old Testament *is* old. But it is still the Bible. As a matter of fact, it is the only Bible Jesus ever read, and he thought it was pretty good. Jesus once said that people who lived the kingdom life and drew from the riches of the Old Testament were like owners of a household who bring out of their "storerooms new treasures as well as old" (Matt. 13:53). Maybe when we say "old," we should see this as meaning that it has abiding value—it has stood the test of time. Since so much of the New Testament is built on the foundation of the Old Testament, maybe we who follow Christ would actually benefit from understanding it.

At Willow Creek Community Church, we decided to take the challenge to read this collection of thirty-nine spiritual classics. The core of our church, what we call "The New Community," agreed together that we'd give it a shot. We devoted a whole ministry year—from September to May—to studying the Old Testament together. As part of that challenge, many of us also used the messages preached as the source of our small-group discussions. And many of us signed on the dotted line to read the Old Testament on our own—*every word*—in forty weeks. As daunting as that sounded, no one who made this commitment and followed through regrets the investment of time. It was truly a once-in-a-lifetime spiritual challenge. It was also a life-transforming forty weeks that blessed each one of us.

So what about you? Are you ready to take the Old Testament Challenge? If so, this guide can help. It divides the Old Testament into approximately equal segments (starting a little slower for the first few weeks) and supports your reading with application questions and an occasional explanatory note. When we used this guide, we didn't just complete the daily assignments; this became the devotional core of our spiritual lives for almost a year. God used these passages in formative ways to make us into a community more like what he's always had in mind for his people. Israel's mistakes were ours to learn from. Their victories were ours to celebrate—and when appropriate, to copy. The songs of the Old Testament have become our songs; its prayers, our prayers. Our hope is that the same will happen for you.

So if you take the challenge—and you've read this far, so you probably will—we want to warn you: God will reveal himself in his Word. You will find, as we did, a God devoted to building a community of faith in the midst of an unbelieving and wayward world. You will discover that God can be a powerful leader or a tender shepherd, an exacting judge or a spurned lover. He might show up as a pillar of fire or a still, small voice. We are confident that you will see, as we did, that despite the centuries and cultural differences, Isaiah was right: "The grass withers and the flowers fall, but the word of our God stands forever" (Isaiah 40:8).

How to Use this Guide

FULL-VERSION READING GUIDE

The "Full-Version" reading guide is divided into roughly forty equal weekly reading assignments. It has been further broken down into daily portions (six each week). For each day there are also reflection questions that are topically connected to something addressed in the text. When phrases from the Bible are quoted in the devotional questions, we used the New International Version. Using that version eliminates possible confusion about what is referred to in a given question. But it is not necessary to use that version for the whole forty weeks. You may want to experiment and read from a variety of translations as you go—or even paraphrases like *The Message*—just to keep the reading fresh.

We understand that most people will not have time in their busy schedules to read the biblical text in addition to other daily devotional guides. That's why, along with the Old Testament text and Psalms, we encourage the use of the personal reflection and application questions included in this book. That way, this reading plan can become a source for your ongoing spiritual formation—not just "homework." The goal is not to *get through the reading* but to *let the reading get through you!* So be sure to take the time to reflect and listen to God speak to you through his Word by using the questions provided, or just meditating on your own.

As a point of clarification, if you are using the full Old Testament Challenge program in your church, the forty-week reading assignment schedule does *not* match up with the topics preached each week. While the small-group curriculum *does* follow the messages exactly, this full version of the reading plan is not designed to be a perfect parallel to the messages and small-group discussions. Some people can be confused by that lack of correspondence. We designed the reading plan this way in order to get through the Old Testament in the allotted forty weeks. You will have to read at a pace that is different from the stories presented in the large-group messages and small-group curriculum. You will be more likely to complete the reading if it is parceled out consistently rather than in widely varying amounts.

FAST-TRACK VERSION

If you are using the Old Testament Challenge material in your church, thirty-two messages cover the whole Old Testament (approximately eight in each kit). If you desire to read passages that relate to the messages being taught each week, the "Fast-Track" plan lays out an abbreviated "high-spots" survey that matches up with the teaching for each week's message.

If you chose this plan, read the selected text and answer the questions *before* the preaching each week as a way to prepare for what will be taught. And if you're in a small group that discusses the material, you'll be that much more prepared for those discussions using the reading and questions provided in the fast-track plan prior to your group meeting.

It's possible you will start doing the full-version reading plan but get bogged down. Don't give up! If you feel as if you just can't cover so much reading in a week, switch to the fast-track plan and finish out using it as your guide. Obviously the best-case scenario is to read everything in God's Word at least once in your lifetime. But wouldn't it be much better to read *something* rather than quit?

Even if you are not doing the Old Testament Challenge in your church, you can use the fast-track plan for a quicker survey of the Old Testament. This is a handy way to familiarize yourself with the great Old Testament themes and key passages. When you're ready, you can come back and use the full version for a comprehensive Old Testament Challenge experience.

Some day, if Zechariah does bump into you in heaven and asks if you enjoyed his book, I hope you can say, "Loved it, Zech! But I have a few questions for you. Can we talk?" I believe that your commitment to take the Old Testament Challenge will have the same life-changing impact on you that it has had on God's people for thousands of years. I pray that God will speak to you in fresh and powerful ways as you open yourself up to his message through this challenge.

—JUDSON POLING

PART 1

READING GUIDE | **Complete Track**

40 WEEK SUMMARY

☐ **WEEK 1** Genesis 1–11; Psalms 1–4	☐ **WEEK 23** 2 Chronicles 1–18; Psalms 78–80
☐ **WEEK 2** Genesis 12–31; Psalms 5–8	☐ **WEEK 24** 2 Chronicles 19–36; Psalms 81–84
☐ **WEEK 3** Genesis 32–50, Psalms 9–12	
☐ **WEEK 4** Exodus 1–20; Psalms 13–17	☐ **WEEK 25** Proverbs 1–15; Psalms 85–88
☐ **WEEK 5** Exodus 21–40; Psalms 18–19	☐ **WEEK 26** Proverbs 16–31; Psalms 89–90
☐ **WEEK 6** Leviticus 1–27; Psalms 20–22	☐ **WEEK 27** Ecclesiastes and Song of Songs; Psalms 91–95
☐ **WEEK 7** Numbers 1–24; Psalms 23–26	☐ **WEEK 28** Isaiah 1–22; Psalms 96–101
☐ **WEEK 8** Numbers 25–36; Deuteronomy 1–11; Psalms 27–30	☐ **WEEK 29** Isaiah 23–44; Psalms 102–103
☐ **WEEK 9** Deuteronomy 12–34; Psalms 31–34	☐ **WEEK 30** Isaiah 45–66; Psalms 104–105
☐ **WEEK 10** Joshua; Psalms 35–36	☐ **WEEK 31** Psalms 106–107
☐ **WEEK 11** Judges; Psalms 37–38	☐ **WEEK 32** Jeremiah 1–20; Psalms 108–109
☐ **WEEK 12** Ruth; 1 Samuel 1–15; Psalms 39–42	☐ **WEEK 33** Jeremiah 21–46; Psalms 110–114
☐ **WEEK 13** 1 Samuel 16–31; 2 Samuel 1–6; Psalms 43–45	☐ **WEEK 34** Jeremiah 47–52; Lamentations; Ezekiel 1–8; Psalms 115–118
☐ **WEEK 14** 2 Samuel 7–24; Psalms 46–49	☐ **WEEK 35** Ezekiel 9–34; Psalm 119
☐ **WEEK 15** 1 Kings 1–11; Psalms 50–53	☐ **WEEK 36** Ezekiel 35–48; Daniel; Psalms 120–124
☐ **WEEK 16** 1 Kings 12–22; Psalms 54–57	☐ **WEEK 37** Hosea; Joel; Amos; Psalms 125–132
☐ **WEEK 17** Psalms 58–62	☐ **WEEK 38** Obadiah; Jonah; Micah; Nahum; Habakkuk; Zephaniah; Haggai; Psalms 133–137
☐ **WEEK 18** 2 Kings 1–13; Psalms 63–66	
☐ **WEEK 19** 2 Kings 14–25, Psalms 67–69	☐ **WEEK 39** Zechariah; Malachi; Ezra; Psalms 138–144
☐ **WEEK 20** Job 1–21; Psalms 70–72	
☐ **WEEK 21** Job 22–42; Psalms 73–75	☐ **WEEK 40** Nehemiah; Esther; Psalms 145–150
☐ **WEEK 22** 1 Chronicles; Psalms 76–77	

Complete Track

GENESIS 1–11; PSALMS 1–4

MONDAY	Genesis 1; Psalm 1
TUESDAY	Genesis 2–3
WEDNESDAY	Genesis 4; Psalm 2
THURSDAY	Genesis 5–6
FRIDAY	Genesis 7–8; Psalm 3
WEEKEND	Genesis 9–11; Psalm 4

Look for. . .
- God's creation of the universe
- Humanity's rebellion against God
- God's provision for his wayward children
- The ark built and Noah rescued from the Flood
- The Tower of Babel built and a prideful "pseudo-community" dispersed

Activity
This week, you're on a "God-hunt." Imagine you know very little about God. What do these early chapters of the Bible teach you about him? What are his likes and dislikes? How powerful is he? What is his nature? Also, pay attention to what you see of God in your everyday life through such things as answered prayer, experiences of beauty, or a prompting to reach out to someone.

This Week's Prayer
Pray this prayer throughout the week: *"Heavenly Father, I want to know you through your Word and meet you in my life. What do you want to teach me about yourself today?"*

☐ **MONDAY** | God's Good Creation
Genesis 1; Psalm 1

• What hint about the "community-nature" of God (the Trinity) can you see in Genesis 1:2 and 26–27?
• If God is invisible, what do you think "created in the image of God" means?
• How would we all treat each other differently if we really believed we were made in God's image—even *with* all our faults?

☐ **TUESDAY** | God's Breath of Life and the Fall of Humanity
Genesis 2–3

• What clue about our need for community is contained in Genesis 2:18? Is a spouse the only solution for this need (hint: 1 John 4:7–8, 12)?
• How did the serpent twist God's words in Genesis 3:1 and 4 (compare Genesis 2:16–17)?
• In spite of the curses, how did God show grace after the Fall? What does this tell you about him?
• What New Testament event does Genesis 3:15 foreshadow?

☐ **WEDNESDAY** | Sin Spreads to Family
Genesis 4; Psalm 2

• In Genesis 4, sin spreads from the individual to the family. How are families you know still experiencing the fallout from sin today?
• In addition to the offering itself, what (or rather, who) was "out of favor" (Genesis 4:4–5)?
• What details from the story of Cain and Abel does Hebrews 11:4 stress?
• What insights about sin's effects do you get from Genesis 4:7?

☐ **THURSDAY** | Sin Spreads Worldwide
Genesis 5–6

• In Genesis 5, the pattern is ". . . and he died" after each person's name—except for what exception in verse 24?
• What does Hebrews 11:5 say about Enoch's special status?
• What was true about Noah that made him the exception to the rest of the world?
• Why do you suppose God waited so long (120 years) to begin the Flood after telling Noah it was coming?
• What does it tell you about God's character that so many years went by before he judged sin? How are you doing these days mimicking God's patience even when retribution is justified?

□ **FRIDAY** | The Flood
Genesis 7–8; Psalm 3

- The ark was one and a half football fields long, holding the volume of 569 railroad cars. Imagine yourself building such a huge structure—and so far away from any body of water, with hostile neighbors watching!
- What do you think might be the significance of who closed the ark (Genesis 7:16)? Does this teach you anything about God?
- What do you learn from these New Testament passages that comment on Noah and the Flood: Hebrews 11:7; 1 Peter 3:18–22; 2 Peter 2:5; and Matthew 24:37–39?
- What was God's response to Noah's offering (Genesis 8:20–22)?

□ **WEEKEND** | God's Covenant; Tower of Babel
Genesis 9–11; Psalm 4

- What covenant did God make with Noah and his descendants in Genesis 9:8–17? What did Noah have to do? What insight does this give you about God's nature?
- What were the purposes for the tower in Genesis 11:4?
- Compare Genesis 9:7; Psalm 2; and Isaiah 14:12–15. What sins do you think were committed by the people who built this monument?
- How does such pride and rejection of God's rule show up in our day? In what ways are you tempted to build your own monument to "Almighty Me"?

THIS WEEK'S NOTES AND REFLECTIONS

_____
_____
_____
_____
_____
_____
_____
_____
_____
_____
_____
_____

OTC

Complete Track

MONDAY	Genesis 12-15; Psalm 5
TUESDAY	Genesis 16-18
WEDNESDAY	Genesis 19-21; Psalm 6
THURSDAY	Genesis 22-24
FRIDAY	Genesis 25-26; Psalm 7
WEEKEND	Genesis 27-31; Psalm 8

Look for...

- The call of Abram (Abraham) to begin a "new community"
- Sodom and Gomorrah destroyed
- Promised son Isaac born
- Isaac "sacrificed" and returned
- Rivalry between twin grandsons Jacob and Esau
- Jacob's "stairway to heaven" dream

Activity

This week, continue your "God-hunt" from last week. What are these early chapters of the Bible teaching you about God's nature? Where do you see God in your everyday life through such things as answered prayer, experiences of beauty, or a prompting to reach out to someone?

This Week's Prayer

Pray this prayer throughout the week: *"Heavenly Father, I want to know you through your Word and meet you in my life. What do you want to teach me about yourself today?"*

☐ MONDAY | God's Covenant with Abraham
Genesis 12–15; Psalm 5

- Though Abram was "chosen" out of the nations, whom else did God want to bless through his offspring (Genesis 12:2–3)? Compare this "Old Testament Great Commission" to the New Testament version in Matthew 28:18–20.
- What "saved" Abram according to Genesis 15:6? (Romans 4 and Galatians 3:6–14 are Paul's inspired commentary on this passage.)
- How does experiencing God's favor inspire us to reach others with that love? Why do we sometimes lose concern for the lost?

☐ TUESDAY | Ishmael Born, Sarai Languishes—and Laughs
Genesis 16–18

- Archaeology shows that Sarai's suggestion in Genesis 16:2 was a common practice in that era; in other words, she was taking her cue from secular culture—with disastrous results. How do we also sometimes miss God's best, rationalizing that "everybody's doing it"?
- What parallels can you make between Sarai's attempt to "help" God and our attempts to force God's will?
- What spiritual parallel to this story is made in Galatians 4:21–31?

☐ WEDNESDAY | Destruction and Birth
Genesis 19–21, Psalm 6

- What does Genesis 19:6–8, 16, 26 and 31–38 tell you about the corrupting influence of this culture on Lot and his family?
- Based on what you've seen of Abraham and Sarah's maturity and faithfulness, what is the significance of the word "gracious" in Genesis 21:1? What do you learn about God from this passage?
- What wordplay is made on Isaac's name (which means "laughter") in Genesis 21:6 going back to 18:10–15?

☐ THURSDAY | Isaac Gets Life—and Later a Wife
Genesis 22–24

- Genesis 22 contains a powerful *type* or metaphor for the future sacrifice and resurrection of God's other "miracle" son, Jesus.
- What parallels in language and imagery do you see between the sacrifice of Isaac and the sacrifice of Jesus in Hebrews 11:17–19; John 3:16; and Romans 8:32?
- Most scholars believe Mount Moriah (Genesis 22:2) is where the temple in Jerusalem was later built (see 2 Chronicles 3:1); today, Islam's beautiful "Dome of the Rock" stands there.

• What kind of conflicting feelings do you suppose Abraham struggled with? What would it take for you to have such confidence in God?

☐ FRIDAY | Esau Sells His Birthright
Genesis 25–26; Psalm 7

• Malachi 1:2–5 harks back to God's kindness to Jacob over Esau as a warning not to be smug. Have you ever felt spiritually complacent because you know God loves you? How can that be avoided?
• Paul notes in Romans 9:6–16 how the scheming Jacob was blessed in spite of his character defects. What lesson about God—and grace—do you take to heart from that fact?
• What additional comments on Esau's foolishness do you find in Hebrews 12:16–17?

☐ WEEKEND | Jacob's Dream and Doublecross; Jacob Flees
Genesis 27–31; Psalm 8

• How did Jesus use the story of Jacob's dream (Genesis 28:10–19) to describe his own role as a "bridge" between God and humans (John 1:50–51)?
• What insight does Genesis 29:20 give about the power of romantic love?
• Notice that Jacob, the deceiver, almost loses his wife because of her deception of him (Genesis 31:32). How does this illustrate Galatians 6:7?
• What is the purpose of the stones and the pledge made in Genesis 31:48–50? (This verse is sometimes taken out of context and used on jewelry—hardly appropriate when you learn the meaning!)

THIS WEEK'S NOTES AND REFLECTIONS

_____

_____

_____

_____

_____

_____

_____

_____

_____

_____

OTC

Complete Track

GENESIS 32-50, PSALMS 9-12

MONDAY	Genesis 32-34; Psalm 9
TUESDAY	Genesis 35-36
WEDNESDAY	Genesis 37-39; Psalm 10
THURSDAY	Genesis 40-41
FRIDAY	Genesis 42-44; Psalm 11
WEEKEND	Genesis 45-50; Psalm 12

Look for...

- Jacob's name changed to Israel
- Jacob's son Joseph (of *Amazing Technicolor® Dreamcoat* fame) dreams of greatness
- Joseph sold by his brothers into slavery
- Joseph's strong stand against Potiphar's wife
- Despite setbacks, Joseph rises to power in Egypt
- Journey of Israel (Jacob) and sons to Egypt and reconciliation with Joseph

Activity

Continue your "God-hunt" from previous weeks. What are these early chapters of the Bible teaching you about God's nature? Where do you see God in your everyday life through such things as answered prayer, experiences of beauty, or a prompting to reach out to someone?

This Week's Prayer

Pray this prayer throughout the week: *"Heavenly Father, I want to know you through your Word and meet you in my life. What do you want to teach me about yourself today?"*

☐ MONDAY | Jacob Wrestles with God
Genesis 32–34; Psalm 9

- What have you seen in Jacob's life that explains his mindset in Genesis 32:7?
- By contrast, what faith lessons do you learn as you read his prayer in Genesis 32:9–12?
- The "man" Jacob wrestles with is clearly a supernatural being, who reminds Jacob that his ultimate struggle isn't with Laban or Esau but with God.
- If you were to "wrestle with God," what would be the issue?

☐ TUESDAY | Safe Return Home
Genesis 35–36

- God changed Jacob's name to Israel (Genesis 32:28; 35:10), a rite of passage signifying his change from "he who deceives" to "he who strives with God."
- What would God have named you before you were his child? What would he name you now?
- How does today's reading—with its long list of names—highlight God at work fulfilling his promise to Abraham in Genesis 12:2; 13:16; and 15:5?

☐ WEDNESDAY | Joseph
Genesis 37–39; Psalm 10

- Do you think Joseph's sense of destiny came from God or from himself?
- What role do you think parental favoritism had (Genesis 37:3–4)—good and bad—in defining Joseph's character?
- Joseph receives two "demotions"; yet how does God work even in those injustices (Genesis 37:2–7 and 20–23)? What does this teach you about God's power—both extent and limitations—in the face of evil?

☐ THURSDAY | Joseph the Interpreter
Genesis 40–41

- What do you think is the difference between what a so-called psychic gives and the interpretation of dreams Joseph offered (Genesis 40:8 and 41:16)?
- What strong warnings concerning those who interpret dreams are given in Deuteronomy 13:1–5 and 18:9–13?
- What other leadership qualities did Joseph exhibit (Genesis 41:33–40)?
- How does Acts 7:9–10 summarize these events?

☐ **FRIDAY** | ## The Famine
Genesis 42–44; Psalm 11

- It's been almost twenty years since Joseph left his brothers. How does his test of their loyalty to their younger brother, Benjamin, compare and contrast to how they treated Joseph years earlier?
- How does Joseph's test uncover changes in his brothers?
- In what way has Genesis 37:5–11 come true at this point in the story?

☐ **WEEKEND** | ## Joseph and Jacob Reunited; Final Blessings
Genesis 45–50; Psalm 12

- What conclusions can you draw from Genesis 45:5–8 and 50:19–20 about God's abilities to use evil people's actions?
- Do you agree or disagree: Evil should *not* be resisted because God can work through it?
- Jacob's blessings (Genesis 49:1–28) are not so much a prediction of what *must* happen to each son as they are a father's observations about each one's character. Through these blessings, Jacob helps his sons see themselves and directs them toward what is good.
- How can parents "bless" their children in a similar fashion today?

THIS WEEK'S NOTES AND REFLECTIONS

OTC

EXODUS 1-20; PSALMS 13-17

MONDAY	Exodus 1-3; Psalms 13-14
TUESDAY	Exodus 4-6
WEDNESDAY	Exodus 5-9; Psalm 15
THURSDAY	Exodus 10-12
FRIDAY	Exodus 13-14; Psalm 16
WEEKEND	Exodus 15-20; Psalm 17

Look for...
- Hebrews (Israelites) becoming slaves
- Moses, a Hebrew, raised as a son of Pharaoh
- Moses and the burning bush
- Ten plagues
- The first Passover
- Manna, quail, and water miraculously supplied in the desert
- The Ten Commandments

Activity
Continue your "God-hunt" from previous weeks. What are these early chapters of the Bible teaching you about God's nature? Where do you see God in your everyday life through such things as answered prayer, experiences of beauty, or a prompting to reach out to someone?

This Week's Prayer
Pray this prayer throughout the week: *"Heavenly Father, I want to know you through your Word and meet you in my life. What do you want to teach me about yourself today?"*

□ **MONDAY** | ## God's Covenant
Exodus 1–3; Psalms 13–14

- What do you think it means to "fear" God as in Exodus 1:17, 21?
- God can only define himself in terms of himself ("I AM WHO I AM"); what is the implication when Jesus defines himself as he does in John 8:56–59?

□ **TUESDAY** | ## God Promises Deliverance
Exodus 4–6

- What similarities exist between how God uses miracles in Exodus 4:1–9 (to authenticate Moses' message) and how Jesus uses miracles in John 2:18–23; 10:25–26 and 37–38?
- What parallel can you make to your own life concerning God's words in Exodus 4:10–12?
- In Exodus 6:1–8, the statement "I am the LORD" is repeated four times; what does God reveal to Moses about himself in response to his complaints?
- What would hearing God say "I am the LORD" mean to you as you face your current challenges?

□ **WEDNESDAY** | ## Knowing God Leads to Obedience
Exodus 5–9; Psalm 15

- How does Exodus 7:22 contradict the assumption that a "miracle" must always come from God (see also Deuteronomy 13:1–4)?
- How did God show his faithfulness to the Israelites in Exodus 8:23 and 9:4, 26? Does God always do this (Matthew 5:45)?

□ **THURSDAY** | ## Pharaoh's Hardened Heart; the Passover
Exodus 10–12

- How did God plan to use Pharaoh's hard heart in Exodus 10:1–2?
- Did God *force* Pharaoh's heart—against Pharaoh's will—to become hard (see Exodus 7:13, 22–23; 8:15, 19, 32; 9:7, 34)?
- What does the Passover represent and why was it to be remembered (Exodus 12:26–27)?
- How did God provide for the Israelites as they left Egypt (Exodus 12:35–36)? How might their years of slavery justify that provision?

☐ **FRIDAY** | ## Consecration of the Firstborn; Crossing the Sea
Exodus 13–14; Psalm 16

- What is the purpose of consecrating the firstborn (Exodus 13:9–16)?

- How do you think your life would change if you saw God part the Red Sea (Exodus 14:31)? Would you ever doubt God again?

- What insight does the Israelites' experience in Exodus 16:3 give as to the convincing power of a miracle (see also Luke 16:31)? What else do people need to be "convinced" and stay faithful to God over time?

☐ **WEEKEND** | ## God's Provision in the Desert; The Ten Commandments
Exodus 15–20; Psalm 17

- After some initial excitement about God's power (Exodus 15:3–11), the Israelites soon grumble about their adversity in the desert; do you think you'd behave the same way in such circumstances?

- Exodus 15:26 states God will heal all the Israelites' diseases. Is this always true for God's people (see Job 2:7–10; 2 Corinthians 12:7–10; Philippians 2:25–30; 1 Timothy 5:23)?

- Is there a situation in your life, work, or ministry where Jethro's advice to Moses in Exodus 18:17–23 could be applicable?

- The people were afraid of God's power, but in Exodus 20:18–20 Moses said they shouldn't be; how should God's power affect us today? What about times when we *don't* see it?

THIS WEEK'S NOTES AND REFLECTIONS

_____

_____

_____

_____

_____

_____

_____

_____

_____

OTC

Complete Track

EXODUS 21-40; PSALMS 18-19

MONDAY	Exodus 21-23; Psalm 18
TUESDAY	Exodus 24-26
WEDNESDAY	Exodus 27-29
THURSDAY	Exodus 30-32; Psalm 19
FRIDAY	Exodus 33-34
WEEKEND	Exodus 35-40

Look for. . .

- The ark of the covenant
- Specifications for the tabernacle and worship
- Israel's fall into idolatry with the golden calf
- Moses and God's glory
- Shining of Moses' face
- The glory of the Lord filling the tabernacle

Activity

Continue your "God-hunt" from previous weeks. What are these early chapters of the Bible teaching you about God's nature? Where do you see God in your everyday life through such things as answered prayer, experiences of beauty, or a prompting to reach out to someone?

This Week's Prayer

Pray this prayer throughout the week: *"Heavenly Father, I want to know you through your Word and meet you in my life. What do you want to teach me about yourself today?"*

☐ MONDAY | Various Laws
Exodus 21–23; Psalm 18

- While these laws may seem harsh by modern standards, what compassionate aspects do you see in Exodus 21:1; 23:1–3, 6, 9?
- The law of retribution ("eye for eye, tooth for tooth, etc.") sets *limits*; it puts a *cap* on liabilities, thus restraining vengeance or greed. How do Jesus' words in Matthew 5:38–42 reinforce this attitude?

☐ TUESDAY | The Ark and the Tabernacle
Exodus 24–26

- Compare Exodus 24:17 with Deuteronomy 4:24 and Hebrews 12:28–29. Why do you think God revealed himself like this, as well as like the image in Exodus 24:9–11?
- All the elements of the tabernacle had two important features: portability and stunning beauty. What might God be teaching the Israelites about his nature through these symbols?

☐ WEDNESDAY | The Priests
Exodus 27–29

- What spiritual lessons might God be teaching through the worship symbols in Exodus 27:21 and 28:29?
- What is the ultimate purpose of the priesthood and its elaborate rituals according to Exodus 29:44–46?

☐ THURSDAY | Craftsmanship; The Golden Calf
Exodus 30–32; Psalm 19

- What is the implication about where the gifts of craftsmanship came from in Exodus 31:1–6?
- What is a contemporary situation similar to what prompted the people to want another god (Exodus 32:1; see also 2 Peter 3:3–4 and Matthew 24:4–13)?
- What lessons about the importance—and limits—of prayer might be learned from Moses' intercession in Exodus 32:11–14 and 30–35?

☐ FRIDAY | God's Presence; New Tablets
Exodus 33–34

- God manifests himself in a variety of ways to teach Moses and his people more about himself. How would you sum up what we learn from his appearances in Exodus 33:9–11, 18–23, and 34:10 and 29–32?

- What do you think the difference is between insecure, selfish "jealousy" and what God has in Exodus 34:14? (Note that the Hebrew word for "zealous" and "jealous" is identical; compare also John 2:13–17 and 2 Corinthians 11:2.)

☐ **WEEKEND** | ## Work on the Tabernacle and the Ark
Exodus 35–40

- Read Exodus 35:20–29. How do you think the experience of community and worship was affected by the widespread participation of individuals?
- Besides being craftsmen, what else did God's Spirit do for Bezalel and Oholiab (Exodus 35:34)?
- What timeless principle can you derive from the Israelites' workmanship and zeal as summed up in Exodus 39:42–43?
- What lesson did the Israelites learn from Exodus 40:36–38? Why do you suppose God stopped leading his people with those sensational means after they entered Canaan? Why do you think he typically doesn't use such dramatic means in our day either?

THIS WEEK'S NOTES AND REFLECTIONS

_____

_____

_____

_____

_____

_____

_____

_____

_____

_____

_____

_____

_____

_____

_____

OTC

Complete Track

LEVITICUS 1-27; PSALMS 20-22

MONDAY	Leviticus 1-5; Psalm 20
TUESDAY	Leviticus 6-9
WEDNESDAY	Leviticus 10-13; Psalm 21
THURSDAY	Leviticus 14-15
FRIDAY	Leviticus 16-19; Psalm 22
WEEKEND	Leviticus 20-27

Look for. . .
- Instructions for five different kinds of offerings (burnt, grain, fellowship, sin, and guilt)
- Priests beginning their ministry
- Violation of God's commands by Nadab and Abihu
- The Day of Atonement (Yom Kippur)
- Instructions for various feasts
- Sabbath Year and Jubilee

Activity
Observe the various laws you obey—or disobey—in the course of an average day (speed limits, paying sales tax, not stealing, voting, etc.). What principles or values can you identify that lie behind the laws? What do you learn about yourself as you react to those laws?

This Week's Prayer
Pray this prayer throughout the week: "Heavenly Father, use your laws to teach me about holiness, reveal my sin, and help me follow you with my whole heart."

☐ MONDAY | Offerings
Leviticus 1–5; Psalm 20

- The book of Leviticus gets its name from *levitikon*, which means *pertaining to the Levites*.
- What insight does Hebrews 7:11 give on the temporary nature of this priestly line?
- How do Ecclesiastes 5:1–7 and Hebrews 4:16 compare and contrast with the basic emphasis of the book of Leviticus (which is that God's chosen people need to approach him in a holy manner)?

☐ TUESDAY | Offerings and the Priesthood
Leviticus 6–9

- How did Moses prepare Aaron and his sons for the priesthood (Exodus 28–29; Leviticus 8)?
- What is the purpose of the anointing oil in Leviticus 8:10–12 and 1 Samuel 16:13 (note: *to anoint* is the root of the Hebrew word *Messiah*—*Christ* in Greek [cf. "christen"])?
- In Leviticus 9:6, God gives a command and promise that he will appear to the Israelites; notice the results in Leviticus 9:23–24. Why do you think God's presence was so powerful at that time?

☐ WEDNESDAY | Nadab and Abihu and Holiness
Leviticus 10–13; Psalm 21

- As the power of God was spectacular in blessing the people (Leviticus 9:24), so it was in punishing the leaders (Leviticus 10:1–3). What do you think justifies God's strong chastisement (see also Acts 5:1–11; James 3:1)?
- God tells his people that they are to be holy because he is holy (Leviticus 10:3; 11:44–45; 19:2; 1 Peter 1:15–16). What does it mean to live a holy life in our day?
- Do you think much about being holy? Why or why not?

☐ THURSDAY | Purification
Leviticus 14–15

- Today's reading shows God's regulations for cleanliness and disease prevention. What principles (such as isolation and sanitation for the prevention of infectious diseases) have timeless—though culturally modified—application for today?
- What might a person living in those days conclude about the level of God's concern for the community?

☐ **FRIDAY** | Day of Atonement
Leviticus 16–19; Psalm 22

- God set forth one day each year for the high priest to represent the whole nation of Israel in a ceremony of atonement (called *Yom Kippur*). What does Hebrews 9 say about this event?
- God expected obedience (Leviticus 18:1–5); yet how is forgiveness—*grace*—provided for? (Hint: notice who "gives" the blood in Leviticus 17:11; also compare Romans 12:1.)
- What is the connection between Leviticus 19:18 and Matthew 22:39?

☐ **WEEKEND** | More Laws and Feasts; Final Tabernacle Preparation
Leviticus 20–27

- A feast is an appointed time to remember a particular event or spiritual lesson; one of the elements of the feasts is a Sabbath, or day of rest, dedicated to the Lord. How can you incorporate "remembering" and taking Sabbaths into your rhythm of life?
- In these chapters, how does the Lord bless the Israelites when they keep his covenant? What are the consequences when they disobey?
- What are some examples of God's grace shown in Leviticus 26?
- What provision is made for a person who sins in Leviticus 26:40–45?

THIS WEEK'S NOTES AND REFLECTIONS

Complete Track

NUMBERS 1-24; PSALMS 23-26

MONDAY	Numbers 1-3; Psalm 23
TUESDAY	Numbers 4-6
WEDNESDAY	Numbers 7-9; Psalm 24
THURSDAY	Numbers 10-13
FRIDAY	Numbers 14-16; Psalm 25
WEEKEND	Numbers 17-24; Psalm 26

Look for. . .
- Complaint of God's people—and getting what they want!
- Miriam and Aaron's undermining of Moses' authority
- Moses' disobedience in anger and his forfeit of living in Canaan
- A bronze serpent on a pole
- Balaam hired to curse Israel
- A talking donkey!

Activity
Observe the various laws you obey—or disobey—in the course of an average day (speed limits, paying sales tax, not stealing, voting, etc.). What principles or values can you identify that lay behind the laws? What do you learn about yourself as you react to those laws?

This Week's Prayer
Pray this prayer throughout the week: *"Heavenly Father, use your laws to teach me about holiness, reveal my sin, and help me follow you with my whole heart."*

☐ **MONDAY** | ## The Census
Numbers 1–3; Psalm 23

- What do you conclude about God as a promise-keeper when you compare Numbers 1:46 with Genesis 22:17?
- What message about spiritual priorities might God be sending by setting apart the able-bodied Levite men to do tabernacle service instead of military (see Numbers 1:45–53)?
- What lesson is God teaching through the relocation of the Tent of Meeting in Numbers 2:17 (compare with Exodus 33:7)?
- Where is God's "tent" in your life these days: more toward the edge, or right in the center? Where do you *want* it to be?

☐ **TUESDAY** | ## Purity and the Nazarite Vow
Numbers 4–6

- What timeless principle about making amends can you get from Numbers 5:6–7?
- Why would it be important for there to be a divinely authenticated method for a woman to prove her innocence in the face of a jealous husband (Numbers 5:14)?
- The Nazirite vow (Numbers 6) typically lasted thirty days (see Acts 18:18; 21:20–24). What do you think is the benefit of a temporary spiritual practice like this?
- It is claimed it takes about thirty days for a new practice to become a habit. What change might God be calling you to instill in your life during the next four weeks?

☐ **WEDNESDAY** | ## Tabernacle Offerings and Cloud
Numbers 7–9; Psalm 24

- Is God's audible voice in Numbers 7:89 the exception or the rule (compare 12:6–8; John 16:13–15; Romans 8:6–9, 14–16)?
- What lessons might be learned by years of "cloud-following" (Numbers 9:15–23)?
- God gives the law, yet expects his people to follow the unpredictable movements of a cloud; how is that similar to how he relates to you?

☐ **THURSDAY** | ## Quail, Fire, Opposition, and Exploration
Numbers 10–13

- What is the *real* problem behind the Israelites' cry in Numbers 11:19–20?
- How are events in Numbers 11:25–29 like Acts 2:14–18 and 19:6?
- What important lesson does Numbers 13:33 contain about how the spies' view of themselves affected their courage?
- Do you see yourself as a "grasshopper" in an area where God sees you differently? How can you see yourself with his eyes?

☐ **FRIDAY** | Rebellion
Numbers 14–16; Psalm 25

- Though God forgave their rebellion, consequences for sin remained (Numbers 14:20–23); what parallels can you make in your own life?
- How do motives and behaviors relate in Numbers 15:25, 30–36?
- Korah used a half truth in Numbers 16:3 to justify rebellion; how have you tried to justify yourself in a similar way?

☐ **WEEKEND** | Moses' Anger; Bronze Serpent; Balaam
Numbers 17–24; Psalm 26

- How is the priesthood a "gift" to Israel (Numbers 18:7)?
- What insight does Psalm 106:32–33 and James 1:19–20 give about Moses' rebellion and anger outburst in Numbers 20:12?
- What do the bronze serpent (Numbers 21:9) and Jesus (John 3:14–15) have in common? How does God save by faith alone in both stories?
- Though Balaam spoke in God's name (Numbers 22–24), how did money taint the whole episode (see 2 Peter 2:15–16; Deuteronomy 18:14)?
- What hidden motives sometimes creep into your outwardly "spiritual" actions?

THIS WEEK'S NOTES AND REFLECTIONS

_____

_____

_____

_____

_____

_____

_____

_____

_____

_____

_____

_____

OTC

Complete Track

NUMBERS 25–36; DEUTERONOMY 1–11; PSALMS 27–30

MONDAY	Numbers 25–27; Psalm 27
TUESDAY	Numbers 28–30
WEDNESDAY	Numbers 31–33; Psalm 28
THURSDAY	Numbers 34–36
FRIDAY	Deuteronomy 1–3; Psalm 29
WEEKEND	Deuteronomy 4–11; Psalm 30

Look for. . .

- Moabites' seduction of Israel
- Joshua to succeed Moses
- Boundaries of Canaan and allotments set
- Levites provided for
- Retelling of wanderings, Ten Commandments
- Motivations and blessings for obedience

Activity

Observe the various laws you obey—or disobey—in the course of an average day (speed limits, paying sales tax, not stealing, voting, etc.). What principles or values can you identify that lay behind the laws? What do you learn about yourself as you react to those laws?

This Week's Prayer

Pray this prayer throughout the week: *"Heavenly Father, use your laws to teach me about holiness, reveal my sin, and help me follow you with my whole heart."*

☐ MONDAY | Moses' Successor Appointed
Numbers 25–27; Psalm 27

- What detail in Numbers 31:16 sheds light on the origins of the seduction of Numbers 25:1–3?
- How would you sum up Joshua's credentials and training to be Moses' successor (Numbers 27:18) from the following verses: Exodus 17:9–13; 24:13; Numbers 11:28; 14:6–9, 30, 36–38?
- What do you think is meant by the symbolism of Moses' laying his hands on Joshua (see Deuteronomy 34:9; Acts 6:6; 1 Timothy 4:14)?
- What do you think of the statement, "There is no success without a successor"? Are you someone's successor? Who is yours?

☐ TUESDAY | Offerings and Vows
Numbers 28–30

- What parallel can you make between the "pleasing aroma" of sacrifices in Numbers 28:2 and Ephesians 5:2 and Hebrews 13:15–16?
- What spiritual principle is taught by insisting sacrifices be "without defect" in Numbers 28:31 (see Malachi 1:13–14)?
- What possible "defective offering" have you been giving God lately? How can you make your sacrifice more worthy of him?
- What is the timeless principle about truth-telling that lies behind the culturally bound instructions of Numbers 30 (hint: see verse 2)?

☐ WEDNESDAY | The Tribes Prepare to Settle Canaan
Numbers 31–33; Psalm 28

- Why is Numbers 31:1–2 not a rule to follow now (see Numbers 31:3 and Romans 12:19–21)?
- What's the timeless principle in Numbers 32:23?
- What effect did the spies' report in Numbers 32:6–15 have on Moses and the national unity at this crucial time?
- How does Numbers 33:55–56 help explain why such extreme measures were necessary during the conquest?

☐ THURSDAY | Boundaries Physical and Legal
Numbers 34–36

- What else do you learn about the cities of refuge in Deuteronomy 19?
- Why do you think there are legal and consequential distinctions between "murder" in Numbers 35:16–21 and "unintentional manslaughter" in 35:22–25?

☐ **FRIDAY** | ## Covenant History
Deuteronomy 1–3; Psalm 29

- The word "Deuteronomy" means "the second giving of the law."
- How do Moses' words in Deuteronomy 3:21–28 help prepare Joshua to carry on after Moses is gone?
- What words can you offer today—based on lessons God has taught you—to help someone face his or her future?

☐ **WEEKEND** | ## Fear, Love, and Serve God
Deuteronomy 4–11; Psalm 30

- Why do the spiritual-sounding human additions to God's law (which produce legalism) in Deuteronomy 4:2 displease God as much as setting aside commands (also see Matthew 15:3–9; 23:4; Revelation 22:18–19; and Eve's additions in Genesis 3:3)?
- What does Jesus say about Deuteronomy 6:4–6 in Matthew 22:37–40?
- Where are spiritual values best modeled according to Deuteronomy 6:7? What happens when they're not modeled there?
- What are parallels in your life to Deuteronomy 8:3, 5, and 18?
- How does Deuteronomy 9:4–6 help explain why the conquest was justified—and why Israel must diligently watch out for the "log in their own eye"?
- What's an application (literal or spiritual) of Deuteronomy 10:18–19 in our day?

THIS WEEK'S NOTES AND REFLECTIONS

OTC

Complete Track

DEUTERONOMY 12-34; PSALMS 31-34

MONDAY	Deuteronomy 12-14; Psalm 31
TUESDAY	Deuteronomy 15-18
WEDNESDAY	Deuteronomy 19-22; Psalm 32
THURSDAY	Deuteronomy 23-26
FRIDAY	Deuteronomy 27-28; Psalm 33
WEEKEND	Deuteronomy 29-34; Psalm 34

Look for...
- Centralized worship commanded
- Tests for false prophets
- Feasts and offerings
- Cities of refuge
- Curses and blessings on Mount Ebal
- Moses' death

Activity
Observe the various laws you obey—or disobey—in the course of an average day (speed limits, paying sales tax, not stealing, voting, etc.). What principles or values can you identify that lay behind the laws? What do you learn about yourself as you react to those laws?

This Week's Prayer
Pray this prayer throughout the week: *"Heavenly Father, use your laws to teach me about holiness, reveal my sin, and help me follow you with my whole heart."*

☐ MONDAY | Worship and Tithes
Deuteronomy 12–14; Psalm 31

- Why does God command not only to avoid idols but also to avoid worshiping God in a pagan fashion (Deuteronomy 12:4 and 29–32)?
- What benefits do you think come from the whole nation periodically worshiping together in one location (Deuteronomy 12:11–14)?
- If a fortune-teller accurately predicts the future but doesn't honor the Bible, how should we respond (based on principles from Deuteronomy 13:1–4)?
- What similarities do you see between Deuteronomy 13:6–8 and Luke 12:51–53 and 14:25–26?

☐ TUESDAY | Legal, Financial, and Ritual Concerns
Deuteronomy 15–18

- What truth helps the Israelites—and us—act generously in Deuteronomy 15:4–6, 10, 14, and 18?
- Jesus alludes to Deuteronomy 15:11 in John 12:8; why would there "always" be poor Israelites if God blesses obedience (see 2 Corinthians 8:13–15 and Philippians 4:12)?
- How does the principle in Deuteronomy 16:17 promote equality (not uniformity) and make giving an occasion to rejoice?
- How is Deuteronomy 17:16–20 borne out many years later in 1 Kings 11?
- How do modern psychics or so-called prophets fare against the test in Deuteronomy 18:21–22?

☐ WEDNESDAY | Capital Punishment, War, Marriage Laws
Deuteronomy 19–22; Psalm 32

- Deuteronomy 19:14 prohibits land theft; what other important legal principle do you find in 19:15?
- Why would distracted soldiers be a liability, according to Deuteronomy 20:5–9?
- What ecological issue drives the commands of Deuteronomy 20:19 and 22:6–7?
- How does Deuteronomy 21:23 shed light on Galatians 3:13?

☐ THURSDAY | Various Laws
Deuteronomy 23–26

- Notice God's further words about Deuteronomy 23:1–2 in Isaiah 56:3–8 (partially fulfilled in *you!*).
- How does grace triumph over Deuteronomy 23:3 in the life of the biblical character Ruth (Ruth 1:16 and 4:17), an ancestor of the Messiah?
- Commercial interest-bearing loans are not forbidden (Deuteronomy 23:19–20; Luke 19:23), but exploiting desperate people is.

- What compassion is engendered by Deuteronomy 23:24–25; 24:12–15, 19–21; and 25:4?

☐ **FRIDAY** | **Blessings and Curses**
Deuteronomy 27–28; Psalm 33

- How did the horrible possibilities in Deuteronomy 28:53–57 actually occur in 2 Kings 6:24–29?
- How do you reconcile Deuteronomy 28:63 with Ezekiel 33:11?

☐ **WEEKEND** | **Covenant Renewed; Moses' Song, Blessing, Death**
Deuteronomy 29–34; Psalm 34

- What bearing does Deuteronomy 29:29 have on unanswered questions in your life (see also John 21:25; Acts 1:7; 1 Corinthians 13:12; 2 Corinthians 4:18)?
- How does the New Testament comment on Moses' ministry in 1 Corinthians 10:1–13; 2 Corinthians 3:7–18; John 1:17; 5:45–47; Acts 13:38–39; and Hebrews 11:24–28?
- In spite of Deuteronomy 32:52 and 34:4, how does God show grace to Moses over 1,400 years later in Matthew 17:3–4?
- What light does Deuteronomy 34:6 shed on Jude 9?
- How is Jesus *the* exception to Deuteronomy 34:10–12 (see Hebrews 3:3–6)?

THIS WEEK'S NOTES AND REFLECTIONS

JOSHUA; PSALMS 35–36

MONDAY	Joshua 1–4; Psalm 35
TUESDAY	Joshua 5–8
WEDNESDAY	Joshua 9–11
THURSDAY	Joshua 12–14; Psalm 36
FRIDAY	Joshua 15–18
WEEKEND	Joshua 19–24

Look for. . .

• Joshua's assumption of leadership: "Be strong and courageous"
• In faith, Rahab the prostitute's hiding of the spies
• The Jordan River miraculously crossed
• Jericho's walls falling down
• The sun standing still
• Land divided
• Joshua's farewell: "As for me and my house. . . ."

Activity

Observe the way living things around you grow and mature: children, pets, plants, and so on. What parallels can you make between their growth—with fits and starts, beauty and bewilderment—and spiritual progress? What most frustrates you about the growth process? What is rewarding?

This Week's Prayer

Pray this prayer throughout the week: *"Heavenly Father, use the history of your people 'growing up' as a nation to teach me how to grow up as your child."*

☐ **MONDAY** | ## Crossing the Jordan
Joshua 1–4; Psalm 35

- The name Joshua (Hebrew *yeh-SHU-ah*; Greek *YAY-sous* or *Jesus*) means, "Yahweh [*or* the LORD] is salvation."
- Which principles in Joshua 1:1–9 still apply today; which don't?
- What marks of "conversion" do you see in Rahab's life in Joshua 2:8–13; Hebrews 11:31; and James 2:25?
- What lesson did God teach "all the peoples" by drying up the Jordan (Joshua 4:20–24)?

☐ **TUESDAY** | ## The Battles of Jericho and Ai
Joshua 5–8

- In Joshua 5:13–15, why would God say he is not an ally (see verse 14)?
- What parallels can you make between God's leading the conquest of Canaan and God's flooding the earth in the time of Noah?
- How does Joshua 6:26 compare with 1 Kings 16:34?
- Which of the Ten Commandments did Achan disobey in Joshua 7:21?
- In the victories at Jericho and Ai, human and divine activities comingle; how is that like the Christian life in our day?

☐ **WEDNESDAY** | ## Deception by Gibeonites; God's Faithfulness
Joshua 9–11

- According to Joshua 9:14, why were the Israelites successfully deceived?
- Do you think the Israelites should have honored their oath in Joshua 9:18–21 even though it was based on a lie?
- Notice how God miraculously gives the Israelites reassurance in chapter 10; then no miracles occur in Joshua 11. How could the Israelites still know that God was with them?
- How do you know God is at work when you can't see it?

☐ **THURSDAY** | ## Dividing the Land; Caleb's Inheritance
Joshua 12–14; Psalm 36

- The roster of names in Joshua 12—though tedious to read—is a reminder of the human powers overthrown by Israel's more powerful God.
- In Joshua 14, after forty-five years, Caleb finally receives his promised inheritance (Numbers 14:6–9, 24; 32:11–12; Deuteronomy 1:35–36). What do you think it would be like to wait four and a half decades while being "wholeheartedly" faithful?

☐ **FRIDAY** | Division of the Land
Joshua 15–18

- How does toleration rather than eradication (Joshua 15:63; 16:10; 17:13) set the stage for fulfillment of Deuteronomy 6:14–15 and Exodus 23:32–33?
- Iron-working gave the Canaanites a technological advantage in weaponry (Joshua 17:16; Judges 1:19; 1 Samuel 4:1–2, 10).
- What insight does Joshua 18:3 give as to why the Israelites took so long to possess the land?

☐ **WEEKEND** | God's Faithfulness; Joshua's Farewell
Joshua 19–24

- What spiritual purpose may God have had in mind by scattering the Levites throughout the land?
- How did Israel's partial obedience affect the benefits of Joshua 21:43–45 (see also Psalm 44:1–3)?
- Read Joshua 22:20; in what ways does sin affect not only the sinner but also innocent bystanders?
- God doesn't commit evil acts (Joshua 23:15; 1 John 1:5), but his justice appears to be "evil" to evil people reaping what they sow (see Titus 1:15). Has God ever seemed "evil" in this way to anyone you know?
- What would today look like if you made the pledge in Joshua 24:15 your own?

THIS WEEK'S NOTES AND REFLECTIONS

_____
_____
_____
_____
_____
_____
_____
_____
_____
_____

OTC

Complete Track

JUDGES; PSALMS 37-38

MONDAY	Judges 1-3; Psalm 37
TUESDAY	Judges 4-5
WEDNESDAY	Judges 6-8
THURSDAY	Judges 9-12; Psalm 38
FRIDAY	Judges 13-16
WEEKEND	Judges 17-21

Look for...

• Cycles of rebellion and deliverance
• Deborah, prophetess and judge
• Gideon's daring exploits
• Jephthah's rash vow
• Samson and Delilah
• "Everyone did as he saw fit" (what was right in his own eyes)

Activity

Observe the way living things around you grow and mature: children, pets, plants, and so on. What parallels can you make between their growth—with fits and starts, beauty and bewilderment—and spiritual progress? What most frustrates you about the growth process? What is rewarding?

This Week's Prayer

Pray this prayer throughout the week: *"Heavenly Father, use the history of your people 'growing up' as a nation to teach me how to grow up as your child."*

☐ **MONDAY** | Othniel and Ehud
Judges 1–3; Psalm 37

- What was the function of a "judge" in this era (Judges 3:9; 4:4–5)?
- Judges 2:10–23 is a brief summary of the whole book.
- Repeated testing (Judges 2:22) was God's way then and now; how does the New Testament bear that out in James 1:2–4 and 1 Peter 4:12–13?
- How is the Spirit being behind Othniel's abilities in Judges 3:10 parallel to Acts 1:8? How is the Spirit similarly active in your life these days?

☐ **TUESDAY** | Deborah
Judges 4–5

- What did it mean to "sell" Israel in Judges 4:2 (see Deuteronomy 32:30)?
- Though Deborah's leadership was rare in a patriarchal society, how do women also play an important leadership role in Exodus 15:20 and 2 Kings 22:14? What might these God-ordained exceptions be telling us about his view of women (see Acts 2:17–18 and Galatians 3:28)?
- The song in Judges 5—like the book of Psalms—fills out God's Word, which not only includes "left-brained" history but also "right-brained" poetry. Why do you think God includes both kinds of teaching in Scripture?

☐ **WEDNESDAY** | Gideon
Judges 6–8

- Do you think Gideon's "putting out a fleece" in Judges 6:35–39 is warranted in light of Judges 6:20–21?
- Soldiers who knelt down to drink (rather than cup water in one hand) laid down their weapons, making themselves vulnerable—perhaps a factor in Judges 7:5–7.
- Even good things, when worshiped, become snares (Judges 8:27; also 2 Kings 18:4; Deuteronomy 5:8–10). What good things in your life can take on such an inflated—and harmful—role?

☐ **THURSDAY** | Abimelech's Rebellion; Jephthah
Judges 9–12; Psalm 38

- God isn't evil (Judges 9:23), but he can use bad people and powers for his purposes (1 Samuel 16:14; 1 Kings 22:19–23; Job 2:3–6; John 6:70–71). How has he done this in your life?
- Though the Spirit is working on Jephthah (Judges 11:29), what foolish "deal" with God did he make in Judges 11:30–31 (see Deuteronomy 12:31; 18:10; 23:21–23; also Leviticus 27:1–8)?
- Have you ever experienced a spiritual "high," soon followed by great folly in your life? What principle in 1 Corinthians 10:12 can help protect you?

☐ **FRIDAY** | ## Samson
Judges 13–16

- Samson was a Nazirite; Numbers 6 teaches about the Nazirite vow—temporary in most cases, lifelong in Samson's (note Luke 1:15 as well).
- How does Judges 13:22 compare with 6:22–23; Genesis 32:30; and Exodus 33:20?
- Samson has been called, "The World's Weakest Strong Man." What aspects of his life bear that out in Judges 14:1–2, 8–9; and 16:1?
- What could happen in your life if you don't strengthen your weak areas?
- How might the Philistines see Samson's capture as vindication for their grain god, Dagon, in Judges 16:23 (cf. 15:4–5)?

☐ **WEEKEND** | ## Micah and the Levite; Benjamites Attacked, Given Wives
Judges 17–21

- What is Micah's character like in Judges 17:4 and 13? How is the Levite portrayed as a corrupt power-seeker in Judges 18:19–20?
- How are Judges 19:22–24 and Genesis 19:4–8 similar?
- How do the events of Judges 19:25–30—among the most horrific in all the Old Testament—bear witness to the effects of Judges 17:6?
- How is the men of Israel's attempt to find a loophole in their vow (Judges 21:1, 20–21) yet another example of the moral deterioration of this era (summarized in Judges 21:25)?
- What teaching in this book do you most need to take to heart in the coming weeks?

THIS WEEK'S NOTES AND REFLECTIONS

OTC

Complete Track

RUTH; 1 SAMUEL 1-15; PSALMS 39-42

MONDAY	Ruth; Psalm 39
TUESDAY	1 Samuel 1-2
WEDNESDAY	1 Samuel 3-5; Psalm 40
THURSDAY	1 Samuel 6-8; Psalm 41
FRIDAY	1 Samuel 9-11; Psalm 42
WEEKEND	1 Samuel 12-15

Look for. . .

- God's faithfulness to a foreigner, Ruth, who joins with his people
- The emergence of Samuel the prophet
- The ark captured by Philistines, with disastrous results
- Israel's rejection of God by asking for a king
- Saul chosen as king
- Saul's half-hearted obedience
- God's rejecting Saul as king

Activity

Observe the way living things around you grow and mature: children, pets, plants, and so on. What parallels can you make between their growth—with fits and starts, beauty and bewilderment—and spiritual progress? What most frustrates you about the growth process? What is rewarding?

This Week's Prayer

Pray this prayer throughout the week: *"Heavenly Father, use the history of your people 'growing up' as a nation to teach me how to grow up as your child."*

☐ MONDAY | Ruth
Ruth; Psalm 39

- As background to this book, the events in Ruth took place during the period of the judges; the Moabites, though not a part of Israel, were descendants of Lot, Abraham's nephew.
- What is a "kinsman-redeemer" (see Ruth 2:20; 3:12; 4:3–6; Leviticus 25:25, 47–49; Deuteronomy 25:5–10)?
- Ruth's faith in God made it possible for her not only to have a place in the community of Israel but also to be an ancestor of David—and eventually of Jesus (Ruth 4:22; Matthew 1:5).
- How does Isaiah 56:1–8 echo God's inclusive love (the theme of this book)?

☐ TUESDAY | Samuel's Birth
1 Samuel 1–2

- What principles of prayer can you glean from Hannah's prayer life in 1 Samuel 1:10–20 and 27–28?
- First Samuel 2:5 says "seven children," though Hannah had only Samuel at that time (and eventually only six total; 1 Samuel 2:21); what does that indicate about biblical use of the number seven (see also Genesis 4:15; Psalm 12:6; Revelation 4:5)?
- How does 1 Samuel 2:26 compare with Luke 2:52?
- What is a modern-day parallel to 1 Samuel 2:17?

☐ WEDNESDAY | The Ark Captured
1 Samuel 3–5; Psalm 40

- In what way can you cultivate similar attitudes expressed in 1 Samuel 3:10 and 19?
- What common parenting mistake is seen in 1 Samuel 3:13?
- How does 1 Samuel 4:1–11 illustrate that it is more important to take God's side than try to make him take yours?
- In 1 Samuel 5, why do you think the Philistines resisted God even though he showed himself so powerful? What does their reaction tell you about miracles as a foolproof evangelistic tool?

☐ THURSDAY | Return of the Ark, Request for a King
1 Samuel 6–8; Psalm 41

- What was wrong with looking into the ark (1 Samuel 6:19; Numbers 4:20)?
- Samuel, like Eli before him, had disobedient children (1 Samuel 8:3)—a possibility even for godly parents.
- What insight does 1 Samuel 8:20 give as to why wanting a king was a rejection of God (see also 8:7)?

☐ **FRIDAY** | ## Samuel Anoints Saul
1 Samuel 9–11; Psalm 42

- What superficial leadership "qualifications" are seen in 1 Samuel 9:1–2? Why do we sometimes pay attention to those instead of true ones?
- What similarities do you see in 1 Samuel 10:6 and 2 Corinthians 5:17?
- How do Augustine's famous words, "Love God, and do as you please" line up with 1 Samuel 10:7?
- What insight does 1 Samuel 9:21 and 10:21–22 give on Saul's low view of himself? How do you suppose that affected his leadership?

☐ **WEEKEND** | ## Saul's Foolishness; Saul's Impulsive Oath and Rejection
1 Samuel 12–15

- According to 1 Samuel 12:21, why is God against idolatry?
- How is 1 Samuel 13:8–13 a good example of how disobedience can appear "religious"?
- God is still looking for "wholehearted" followers (1 Samuel 13:14); how is your heart these days?
- How did Saul's cover-up in 1 Samuel 15:15 again carry a "religious" cloaking?
- What parallel can you make between 1 Samuel 15:22–23 and Psalm 51:16–17?

THIS WEEK'S NOTES AND REFLECTIONS

Complete Track

1 SAMUEL 16-31; 2 SAMUEL 1-6; PSALMS 43-45

MONDAY	1 Samuel 16-17; Psalm 43
TUESDAY	1 Samuel 18-20
WEDNESDAY	1 Samuel 21-24; Psalm 44
THURSDAY	1 Samuel 25-27
FRIDAY	1 Samuel 28-31; Psalm 45
WEEKEND	2 Samuel 1-6

Look for. . .

- David and Goliath
- David's friendship with Jonathan
- Saul's irrational jealousy, rage, and depression
- David's sparing Saul's life
- Saul's consulting a medium with disastrous results
- Saul's death, David's reign
- David's capturing Jerusalem and making it his capital

Activity

Observe the way living things around you grow and mature: children, pets, plants, and so on. What parallels can you make between their growth—with fits and starts, beauty and bewilderment—and spiritual progress? What most frustrates you about the growth process? What is rewarding?

This Week's Prayer

Pray this prayer throughout the week: *"Heavenly Father, use the history of your people 'growing up' as a nation to teach me how to grow up as your child."*

□ **MONDAY** | David Anointed, Defeats Goliath
1 Samuel 16–17, Psalm 43

- How does 1 Samuel 16:7 compare with the description of the Messiah in Isaiah 53:2–3?
- First Samuel 16:14 may be similar to God's hardening Pharaoh's heart, or a general description of events within God's providence (as in Judges 9:23).
- What victories in your life give you confidence like David had in 1 Samuel 17:37?

□ **TUESDAY** | Saul's Jealousy, Jonathan and David
1 Samuel 18–20

- How is 1 Samuel 18:1–4 a timeless description of deep friendship?
- What do your friendships tell you about your life?
- What is a major difference between the Spirit's work in Old Testament believers (1 Samuel 19:20–23; Numbers 11:24–25; Psalm 51:11) and his indwelling in the New Testament (John 14:17; Romans 8:9; Ephesians 1:13–14)?

□ **WEDNESDAY** | Saul Pursues David
1 Samuel 21–24; Psalm 44

- What principle did Jesus illustrate by quoting (in Luke 6:3–4) the incident in 1 Samuel 21:1–6?
- The "uncleanness" of 1 Samuel 21:5 is ritual, not moral (Leviticus 15:18).
- First Samuel 22:2 describes a ragtag band of losers; why are those the kind of people God uses (1 Corinthians 1:26–29)?
- How is 1 Samuel 24 an illustration of Matthew 5:43–44; Romans 12:19–21; and 1 Peter 2:18–23?

□ **THURSDAY** | Abigail, David Again Spares Saul
1 Samuel 25–27

- In 1 Samuel 25, how does Abigail demonstrate both commendable marital loyalty and destructive marital enabling?
- David honors the office in spite of the man who holds it (1 Samuel 26:9–11). What's a modern analogy to this action?
- Who is a person in your life whom you must respect and yet who has done little to earn it? How can you best respond in a Christlike way?

☐ **FRIDAY** | ## Saul and the Medium; Saul Dies
1 Samuel 28–31; Psalm 45

- Saul's visit with a medium is the last-ditch effort of a desperate man. What has desperation ever driven you to do?
- The "old man" in 1 Samuel 28:14 could be a human or demonic impersonator; either way, Saul's actions are strictly forbidden in Deuteronomy 18:10–11 and Isaiah 8:19–20.
- Saul's armor (1 Samuel 31:10), like Goliath's sword (21:9), is displayed as an emblem of defeat.

☐ **WEEKEND** | ## David Gains Power, Takes Jerusalem
2 Samuel 1–6

- The man lies (2 Samuel 1:10), possibly to get a reward; how *does* he get his reward?
- Though David has been anointed king, he still has to consolidate his power using kind words of thanks (2 Samuel 2:4–7); he engaged in necessary military contests, small (2:13–16) and large (2:1; 7:1–2); he also rejected unjust murder though it could have helped him politically (4:9–12). What analogies can you make to a modern leader stepping into a new role?
- How is touching the ark (2 Samuel 6:6–7) a clear violation of Numbers 4:15? What is something "holy"—person or principle—that you need to treat with greater reverence?
- Enthusiastic worshipers, take heart from David's example (2 Samuel 6:14, 21–22)!

THIS WEEK'S NOTES AND REFLECTIONS

Complete Track

MONDAY	2 Samuel 7-9; Psalm 46
TUESDAY	2 Samuel 10-12; Psalm 47
WEDNESDAY	2 Samuel 13-14
THURSDAY	2 Samuel 15-17; Psalm 48
FRIDAY	2 Samuel 18-19; Psalm 49
WEEKEND	2 Samuel 20-24

Look for...
- David forbidden to build temple
- David and Bathsheba
- David's failures as a father
- Absalom's rebellion and death
- David counting the troops—with disastrous results

Activity
Often we seek God's presence in times of trouble and pain. Yet what about times of pleasure and relative "success"? How do we tend to respond to him then? This week, look for God's presence in the "highs" as you live day to day. Record those positive experiences and reflect on God's involvement with you in each one. How might remembering God in those times influence your responses?

This Week's Prayer
Pray this prayer throughout the week: *"God, teach me to enjoy seasons of blessing in ways that bring me closer to you."*

☐ MONDAY | God's Promise to David; Mephibosheth
2 Samuel 7–9; Psalm 46

- How does 1 Chronicles 22:7–10 more fully explain why God doesn't let David build the temple (2 Samuel 7:13)?
- Second Samuel 7:16 is not an overstatement; how is it fulfilled in Luke 1:31–33 and Hebrews 1:8–9?
- What is David's poetic and theological explanation for 2 Samuel 8:4 in Psalm 20:7?
- How is 2 Samuel 9:1 a fulfillment of David's oath in 1 Samuel 20:12–15?

☐ TUESDAY | David and Bathsheba
2 Samuel 10–12; Psalm 47

- What do 2 Samuel 11:2; Genesis 3:6; and 1 John 2:16 have in common?
- Sin produces a "cover-up" (2 Samuel 11:6–13), leading to murder (2 Samuel 11:15); but what is a biblically guaranteed outcome of *every* cover-up (1 Timothy 5:24)? Have you seen this happen in your own life?
- Nathan's clever confrontation (2 Samuel 12:1–10) has the desired effect (12:13); though God forgives the sin (12:13), what consequences remain (12:14)?
- Though explicit teaching in the Old Testament is rare, how do 2 Samuel 12:23; Deuteronomy 32:50; and Job 19:25–27 hint at the idea of an afterlife?

☐ WEDNESDAY | David's Problem Sons
2 Samuel 13–14

- Lust acted on is never like the fantasy; how does sin indulged disappoint in 2 Samuel 13:15?
- What lessons have you learned about the disappointing effects of sin? What sin is looking good to you—such that you need to keep this story in mind?
- How does David's failure to punish Amnon (2 Samuel 13:21–22) and Absalom (2 Samuel 15:1–6) undermine his leadership?

☐ THURSDAY | Absalom's Rebellion
2 Samuel 15–17; Psalm 48

- What connection can you make between David's eroding self-confidence (2 Samuel 15:14; cf. also calling Absalom "king" in 15:19 and accepting curses in 16:10–11), his forfeiture, with Bathsheba, of moral high ground (12:10–12, fulfilled in 16:22), and years of yielding to his sons' corruption?

☐ **FRIDAY** | **Absalom Defeated**
2 Samuel 18–19; Psalm 49

- How strong is parental love, even in the face of rebelliousness (2 Samuel 18:33)?

- Read Matthew 23:37. How is David's lament an echo of God's anguish for his disobedient sons and daughters?

- What connection might there be between the story of David uncovering Mephibosheth's loyalty (2 Samuel 19:29–30) and Solomon's legendary wisdom (1 Kings 3:16–27)?

☐ **WEEKEND** | **David's Kingdom Reestablished; The Census**
2 Samuel 20–24

- "Wise woman" (2 Samuel 20:15–16; cf. 14:2) may be a title, similar to prophet or "mother in Israel" (20:19; cf. Judges 4:4–5; 5:7). How is this an indication that even in that patriarchal society, God guided women to play an important leadership role?

- The Thirty (2 Samuel 23:24) included thirty-seven men at various times (23:39), much as "the Twelve" eventually included a thirteenth (Acts 1:26).

- First Chronicles 21:1 says Satan, not God, instigated the census (2 Samuel 24:1); how can both evil and divine purposes be at work in the same choices (see John 6:70–71; 13:27; Acts 2:23)? Have you ever seen this in your experience?

- This census is immoral, recognized by Joab and David (2 Samuel 24:3, 10); how does Exodus 30:11–12 help explain David's financial motive?

THIS WEEK'S NOTES AND REFLECTIONS

_____

_____

_____

_____

_____

_____

_____

_____

_____

_____

OTC

Complete Track

1 KINGS 1-11; PSALMS 50-53

MONDAY	1 Kings 1; Psalm 50
TUESDAY	1 Kings 2-3; Psalm 51
WEDNESDAY	1 Kings 4-5; Psalm 52
THURSDAY	1 Kings 6-7
FRIDAY	1 Kings 8; Psalm 53
WEEKEND	1 Kings 9-11

Look for...
- David's making Solomon king and then dying
- Solomon's great wisdom (and at the end of his life, his great folly)
- Solomon's building the first temple and a palace for himself
- Visit of the Queen of Sheba
- Solomon's many wives, who are "religious" but lead him from God

Activity
Often we seek God's presence in times of trouble and pain. Yet what about times of pleasure and relative prosperity and success? How do we tend to respond to him then? This week, look for God's presence in the "highs" as you live day to day. Record those positive experiences and reflect on God's involvement with you in each one. How might remembering God in those times influence your responses?

This Week's Prayer
Pray this prayer throughout the week: "God, teach me to enjoy seasons of blessing in ways that bring me closer to you."

□ **MONDAY** | ## Aged David Makes Solomon King
1 Kings 1; Psalm 50

- How does Adonijah (1 Kings 1:5) copy his brother Absalom (2 Samuel 15:1)?
- How is Bathsheba's role as "first wife" and Solomon's succession as king (1 Kings 1:11–14) a testimony to God's grace—turning sin to something good? When has God done something similar for you?
- What's the connection between 1 Kings 1:33–34; Zechariah 9:9; and Mark 11:1–10?

□ **TUESDAY** | ## Solomon Rules
1 Kings 2–3; Psalm 51

- How is 1 Kings 2:2–3 wise fatherly advice—now as then?
- What light does 2 Samuel 16:20–22 shed on the motives of Adonijah's request in 1 Kings 2:17, 22?
- Marrying for political reasons (1 Kings 3:1), which was common in Bible times, receives a warning from God in Deuteronomy 17:17. What common practices in our day must we take caution against?
- At age twenty, Solomon is only slightly exaggerating (1 Kings 3:7).
- How does 1 Kings 3:10–14 illustrate Matthew 6:33?

□ **WEDNESDAY** | ## Solomon's Wisdom
1 Kings 4–5; Psalm 52

- First Kings 4:20–21, 25 describes Israel at the zenith of power and prosperity, never to be matched again in her history.
- How does Solomon's wisdom extend to nature—God's creation (1 Kings 4:33)?
- What additional New Testament insight into "wisdom" does James 1:5–8 and 3:13–18 contain?
- In Jerusalem today, some of these very stones (1 Kings 5:17) can be seen at the base of the Western Wall.

□ **THURSDAY** | ## Construction of the Temple and Palace
1 Kings 6–7

- Prefitted stones (1 Kings 6:7) make construction quicker, but they also conform to Exodus 20:25 and Joshua 8:31 (iron tools had pagan associations).
- What is the difference between images to be worshiped (Exodus 20:4–5) and images *used in* worship (1 Kings 6:29; 7:18–22, 36)?
- First Kings 6:38–7:1 may contain subtle criticism of Solomon's priorities. In what ways are you putting some of your own interests ahead of God's recently?

☐ **FRIDAY** | Dedication of Temple
1 Kings 8; Psalm 53

- Did somebody "raid the ark"? (Compare 1 Kings 8:9 with Exodus 16:32–34 and Numbers 17:10.)
- How does the New Testament (Acts 7:47–50) agree with Solomon (1 Kings 8:27)?
- In what way is Solomon's prayer "evangelistic" (1 Kings 8:41–43; see also Deuteronomy 4:6 and Genesis 12:3)?
- How does Paul agree with 1 Kings 8:46 in Romans 3:10–18?

☐ **WEEKEND** | Queen of Sheba; Solomon's Pagan Wives
1 Kings 9–11

- Recent archaeological excavations—so-called Solomonic gates—confirm Solomon's renovations in the three cities mentioned at the end of 1 Kings 9:15. How can these discoveries reinforce confidence in the accuracy of the Old Testament?
- How does spiritual—not just temporal—power fulfill God's intentions for Israel and make Solomon renown in 1 Kings 10:1. (Notice Jesus' allusion to this in Matthew 12:42.)
- Did Solomon's wisdom fail, or did he fail to follow wisdom in 1 Kings 11:9–10?
- One piece/tribe is missing in 1 Kings 11:30–32. Possible explanations include: Levi, which has no allotment; Simeon, which is absorbed into Judah; or Benjamin, which is divided between the others.
- As you think of the first three kings—Saul, David, and Solomon—what lessons do you want to apply to your life from each of their lives?

THIS WEEK'S NOTES AND REFLECTIONS

_____

_____

_____

_____

_____

_____

_____

_____

_____

_____

Complete Track

MONDAY	1 Kings 12; Psalms 54-55
TUESDAY	1 Kings 13-14
WEDNESDAY	1 Kings 15-16; Psalm 56
THURSDAY	1 Kings 17
FRIDAY	1 Kings 18-19; Psalm 57
WEEKEND	1 Kings 20-22

Look for. . .

- Israel/Judah divide into two kingdoms
- Golden calf *déjà vu*
- Bad kings multiplying
- Miraculous ministry of Elijah
- Test on Mount Carmel
- Ahab's evil ways

Activity

Often we seek God's presence in times of trouble and pain. Yet what about times of pleasure and relative prosperity and success? How do we tend to respond to him then? This week, look for God's presence in the "highs" as you live day to day. Record those positive experiences and reflect on God's involvement with you in each one. How might remembering God in those times influence your responses?

This Week's Prayer

Pray this prayer throughout the week: *"God, teach me to enjoy seasons of blessing in ways that bring me closer to you."*

☐ MONDAY | Division
1 Kings 12; Psalms 54–55

- After Solomon's death, Israel (north) and Judah (south) become two nations, never again to be a politically united people (but note Ezekiel 37:15–20).
- Age doesn't guarantee wisdom, but why is it folly for Rehoboam to reject his older counselors (1 Kings 12:8; Leviticus 19:32)?
- Even in Rehoboam's sinful choice, how is God at work in 1 Kings 12:15; 11:29–33?
- Compare 1 Kings 12:28 with Exodus 32:4; what political ends cause the spiritual compromise (1 Kings 12:27)?

☐ TUESDAY | Prophets and Prophecy
1 Kings 13–14

- "Man of God" (1 Kings 13:1; 12:22) is synonymous with what Old Testament office?
- As in 1 Kings 13:18, many in our day also claim to have a message from God; what are some truth tests? (Hint: see Isaiah 8:19–20; Jeremiah 23:21–22, 25–29; 1 John 4:1–3; 2 John 7–9; and Galatians 1:6–9.)
- How is pagan worship (1 Kings 14:23–24) a way of "hedging your bets" in case God doesn't come through? Why might the sexual aspects of such "worship" also hold an appeal?
- How are you tempted to rely on forbidden things as a way to provide for yourself "in case God doesn't"?

☐ WEDNESDAY | Bad Kings
1 Kings 15–16; Psalm 56

- What insight does 2 Chronicles 16:7–9 give on the sin behind Asa's treaty in 1 Kings 15:18–19?
- The litany of bad kings climaxes with Ahab (1 Kings 16:30–33).
- What judgment of God (Joshua 6:26) proved true in the case of Hiel in 1 Kings 16:34?
- Do you think God curses disobedience, or is disobedience its own curse? What have you seen in your own life to support your answer?

☐ THURSDAY | Elijah and the Widow
1 Kings 17

- What does James 5:17–18 say about 1 Kings 17:1?
- How does God's mercy to a non-Jew in 1 Kings 17:9–16 show his intent to reach out to Gentiles and illustrate his gracious choice of unworthy sinners? (Note also Jesus' comments in Luke 4:25–26.)
- What are similarities between 1 Kings 17:21 and Acts 20:9–12?
- Beyond compassion, why do you think God does miracles like the ones above? For what reasons might he refrain from doing miracles?

☐ **FRIDAY** | Test on Mount Carmel
1 Kings 18–19; Psalm 57

- Elijah's sarcasm is biting, but revealing (1 Kings 18:27). Read this verse in several translations for a fuller appreciation of the Hebrew idiom.
- How does the story in 1 Kings 18:28–29 demonstrate that "sincerity" in religion is not enough? How do Paul's words in Romans 10:2 shed light on what else is needed?
- How is Baal, the god of water, further humiliated by God's power in 1 Kings 18:33–35, 38?
- What surprising mood follows Elijah's great ministry triumph in 1 Kings 19:4–5? Have you ever experienced this? (If so, you're in good company!)

☐ **WEEKEND** | Ahab Wins Battle, Rejects Warning, and Dies
1 Kings 20–22

- How does the acted-out parable in 1 Kings 20:38–42 illustrate Ahab's disregard for God's deliverance (20:28) and the error of freeing Ben-Hadad? How is Nathan's technique similar in 2 Samuel 12:1–12?
- Ahab's repentance seems sincere and God declares it so in 1 Kings 21:27–29; yet how does he show contempt for another prophet in 1 Kings 22:8?
- Do you think Micaiah is being sarcastic in 1 Kings 22:15? (Note Ahab's response in v. 16.)
- First Kings 22:19–23 may be a figurative event, meant to teach the point; which way does Ahab go when God offers him a choice?
- Can a disguise (1 Kings 22:30) alter God's prediction (22:28, 34, 37)?

THIS WEEK'S NOTES AND REFLECTIONS

_____

_____

_____

_____

_____

_____

_____

_____

_____

_____

Complete Track

PSALMS 58–62

Catch Up Week

This week is a catch-up week. If you've fallen behind in the reading, use this time to get caught up. If you're on track, read whatever you like—and enjoy the break! Either way, the only additional assignment this week is to read Psalms 58–62.

Next week, you'll resume your regular daily reading schedule.

Complete Track

2 KINGS 1–13; PSALMS 63–66

MONDAY	2 Kings 1–2; Psalm 63
TUESDAY	2 Kings 3–4
WEDNESDAY	2 Kings 5–6; Psalm 64
THURSDAY	2 Kings 7–8
FRIDAY	2 Kings 9–10; Psalm 65
WEEKEND	2 Kings 11–13; Psalm 66

Look for. . .

- Elijah taken to heaven in a chariot of fire
- Miracles of provision, resurrection, protection, healing
- Marauding Arameans miraculously struck with blindness
- Famine and deliverance at Samaria
- Jezebel killed
- Lone descendant of David protected
- Death of Elisha

Activity

The kings of Israel and Judah often used their power in corrupt ways, though they did not have to. This week, notice settings in which you are powerful—or could be. Guided by the Holy Spirit, use your power to cheer a friend, influence a child, take a stand for integrity, or encourage a coworker. Intentionally live out Proverbs 3:27: "Do not withhold good from those who deserve it, when it is in your power to act."

This Week's Prayer

Pray this prayer throughout the week: *"God, show me my power, use it for good, and protect me from pride."*

☐ **MONDAY** | ### Elijah Succeeded by Elisha; Chariots of Fire
2 Kings 1–2; Psalm 63

- The actual name of the god in 2 Kings 1:2 is Baal-Zebul, "lord, the prince," but the Israelites tauntingly called him Baal-Zebub, "lord of the flies." Jesus uses this false god's name as a mockery of Satan in Matthew 12:24.
- What comparisons can you make between Elijah and John the Baptist (2 Kings 1:8; Matthew 3:4; 17:11–13; Luke 1:17)?
- Elijah's miraculous end (2 Kings 2:11) foreshadows what miraculous events in the messianic era (Malachi 4:5–6; Luke 9:28–33; possibly Revelation 11:3–12)?

☐ **TUESDAY** | ### Elisha's Supernatural Provisions
2 Kings 3–4

- What were the "sins of Jereboam" (2 Kings 3:3) according to 1 Kings 12:28–33?
- Is "sincere" idolatry justified (2 Kings 3:27)?
- God's miracles sometimes conform to humanly imposed limits; how big are the "containers" you're giving him to fill (2 Kings 4:3–6; John 2:6–11)?
- What parallels do you see between 2 Kings 4:42–44 and John 6:5–14?

☐ **WEDNESDAY** | ### Naaman Healed
2 Kings 5–6; Psalm 64

- Disease is not a sign of God's disfavor (2 Kings 5:1), yet God sometimes does heal this side of heaven (2 Kings 5:13–14); in the end, all will be healed (Revelation 22:1–3).
- Naaman associates God with the land of Israel (2 Kings 5:17); what would Jesus say (John 4:19–24)?
- How serious is lying to God (2 Kings 5:23–27; Acts 5:1–11)?
- How are spiritual realities in some ways more *real* than physical (2 Kings 6:15–17; 2 Corinthians 4:16–18)?

☐ **THURSDAY** | ### Siege Ends; Ben-Hadad Murdered
2 Kings 7–8

- How is the lepers' realization (2 Kings 7:9) like our assignment to share spiritual good news (2 Timothy 4:1–2; Matthew 5:14–16; Acts 1:8)?
- How does 2 Kings 8:19 in part explain God's patience with evil (see 2 Peter 3:9 for another reason)?
- The tension of 2 Kings 8:22 carries over into the New Testament, where the Herods (Matthew 2:1; 14:1; Acts 12:2; 23), descendents of Edom, rule Israel by Roman decree.

☐ **FRIDAY** | Jehu
2 Kings 9–10; Psalm 65

- Notice Jehu's mixed up spiritual priorities. What positive stand does he take in 2 Kings 9:22; 10:25–28, yet what compromise does he make in 2 Kings 10:29?
- What good thing does Jehu do in an evil way in 2 Kings 10:18–19?
- Why is it important for us to be consistent in our obedience—and to pay attention to *how* we do what we do?

☐ **WEEKEND** | Joash; Elisha's Last Days
2 Kings 11–13; Psalm 66

- Joash (2 Kings 11:1–3) was the only survivor to the line of David; had he been killed, what would have happened to Messiah ("son of David/Jesse," cf. 2 Samuel 7:16; Jeremiah 23:5–6; Ezekiel 34:22–24; Isaiah 11:1–10)?
- Jehoahaz sought God's help but not God's holiness (2 Kings 13:2–6); how is that like many in our day?
- Jehoash's halfhearted response (2 Kings 13:18) evidenced a halfhearted devotion.
- What purpose might a physical object serve when God does a miracle (2 Kings 13:21; John 9:6–7; Acts 19:11–12)?

THIS WEEK'S NOTES AND REFLECTIONS

_____

_____

_____

_____

_____

_____

_____

_____

_____

_____

_____

_____

OTC

Complete Track

2 KINGS 14-25, PSALMS 67-69

MONDAY	2 Kings 14-15; Psalm 67
TUESDAY	2 Kings 16-17
WEDNESDAY	2 Kings 18; Psalm 68
THURSDAY	2 Kings 19
FRIDAY	2 Kings 20-22; Psalm 69
WEEKEND	2 Kings 23-25

Look for. . .

- Samaria (northern kingdom) destroyed by Assyria (722 B.C.)
- Moses' bronze snake worshiped, destroyed
- Righteous kings Hezekiah and Josiah seeking God
- God's Law book found during temple remodeling
- Judah (southern kingdom) destroyed by Babylon (586 B.C.)

Activity

The kings of Israel and Judah often used their power in corrupt ways, though they did not have to. This week, notice settings in which you are powerful—or could be. Guided by the Holy Spirit, use your power to cheer a friend, influence a child, take a stand for integrity, or encourage a coworker. Intentionally live out Proverbs 3:27: "Do not withhold good from those who deserve it, when it is in your power to act."

This Week's Prayer

Pray this prayer throughout the week: "God, show me my power, use it for good, and protect me from pride."

☐ **MONDAY** | Kings of Israel and Judah
2 Kings 14–15; Psalm 67

- This is the same Jonah (2 Kings 14:25) who was swallowed by a big fish.
- What is happening to the northern kingdom of Israel (2 Kings 15:29)?
- Uzziah (2 Kings 15:30) is Azariah, possibly the former his royal title and the latter his name.
- Several leaders of Israel are summed up in these chapters by a sentence or two; how would *your* one-sentence life summary read?

☐ **TUESDAY** | Samaria/Northern Israel Falls
2 Kings 16–17

- Impressed with the Assyrian king's power, Ahaz does what forbidden—but "spiritual" sounding—act (2 Kings 16:10)?
- Ahaz also used the altar (2 Kings 16:15) for worthless—and forbidden—divination (that is, looking for clues to the future by examining organs of sacrificed animals).
- Was Uriah (2 Kings 16:16) always so compromised (Isaiah 8:1–2)?
- Notice the sad summary of Samaria's (northern Israel's) legacy in 2 Kings 17:7–23.
- Did the compromises of those who resettled Samaria (2 Kings 17:33–34)—hated even in Jesus' time—put them beyond God's redemptive love (John 4:9, 19–27)?

☐ **WEDNESDAY** | Hezekiah and Sennacherib
2 Kings 18; Psalm 68

- What symbol of deliverance was defiled by the idolatrous nature of the people (2 Kings 18:4; see Numbers 21:8–9)?
- Sennacherib uses every device he can to taunt the inhabitants of Jerusalem, including the claim he is from the Lord their God (2 Kings 18:25); ironically, he's half-right, for God *was* using him as a tool (2 Kings 18:12) though he didn't know it.
- Has God ever used someone else's evil acts as a tool to shape you for the better?

☐ **THURSDAY** | Hezekiah's Prayer and Jerusalem's Deliverance
2 Kings 19

- What terrible news (2 Kings 18:14–19) do you need to "spread out" before the Lord? He will hear your prayer too!
- Isaiah's prophecy (2 Kings 19:20–34) as well as this history is found in Isaiah 37:21–35.
- This plague is mentioned in nonbiblical historical sources (Josephus), and Assyrian archaeology mentions the siege—but not the capture—of Jerusalem.

□ **FRIDAY** | **Hezekiah's Life Extended; Manasseh's Evil**
2 Kings 20–22; Psalm 69

- Hezekiah's prayer is answered (2 Kings 20:5–6), yet as with Israel's request for a king, how is the result a mixed blessing (2 Kings 21:1–17; see 2 Kings 20:1 for God's first word to him)?

- God's Word (probably the book of Deuteronomy) survives years of evil leadership (2 Kings 22:8); when found and applied, it starts a revival (2 Kings 22:11; 23). What parallels can you make to how his Word works in our day?

- Rare in a patriarchal culture, God sometimes uses women as his spokespersons (2 Kings 22:14; see also Exodus 15:20; Isaiah 8:3); what might this signify about his ultimate design for humanity (Joel 2:28–29; Galatians 3:28)?

□ **WEEKEND** | **Josiah's Reforms; Fall of Jerusalem; Captivity**
2 Kings 23–25

- Meggido is a famous battlefield (2 Kings 23:29), the basis for the word "Armageddon" (Revelation 16:16).

- Though God may cause a nation to bear sin's consequences (2 Kings 24:4; 25:21), what promise is offered to any who ask *individually* for forgiveness (Ezekiel 18:27–32; Micah 7:18–19; Isaiah 1:18, 27)?

THIS WEEK'S NOTES AND REFLECTIONS

_____

_____

_____

_____

_____

_____

_____

_____

_____

_____

_____

_____

OTC

JOB 1-21; PSALMS 70-72

MONDAY	Job 1-4; Psalm 70
TUESDAY	Job 5-7
WEDNESDAY	Job 8-10; Psalm 71
THURSDAY	Job 11-13
FRIDAY	Job 14-17; Psalm 72
WEEKEND	Job 18-21

Look for. . .

- Satan's accusation of Job regarding a "fair-weather friendship" with God
- God's allowing—and limiting—Satan's testing of Job
- Job's faith mocked by his wife
- Job's friends falsely accusing Job of wrongdoing
- Job's maintaining his integrity and his cry to be vindicated

Activity

Pay attention to what people do to help those who suffer. What words are used? What actions are taken? What words and actions seem to truly help? What words and actions make the problem worse?

This Week's Prayer

Pray this prayer throughout the week: *"God, show me how to help those who suffer without sounding like Job's friends."*

☐ **MONDAY** | ## Prologue and Testing
Job 1–4; Psalm 70

- Satan's accusation (Job 1:9–11) echoes through the ages: Do we love God only because of his benefits, or for who he is? How does your life answer that question?
- What do the limits put on Satan (Job 1:12; 2:6) tell you about God's power—and Satan's?
- What did Job's friends do right in Job 2:13? Why do you think we often feel the need to talk instead of just "be with" those in pain?

☐ **TUESDAY** | ## Eliphaz Speaks, Job Replies
Job 5–7

- Here's a tip for understanding this book: In Job 42:7, God says that things spoken by Job's friends are wrong; Job himself admits many of his words were wrong as well (42:2–6). Therefore, this book contains lots of theological errors—correctly recorded! No statement of Job or especially of his friends should be assumed as good theology without corroboration elsewhere in Scripture (some examples to be "questioned": 5:12; 6:14; 7:7, 15–16).
- Job 7:17 sounds like Psalm 8:4, but how does Job 7:18 shows the extent of Job's reinterpretation of Psalm 8:5?

☐ **WEDNESDAY** | ## Bildad Speaks, Job Replies
Job 8–10; Psalm 71

- Notice the ironies in Job 8:4–7; Job *did* offer sacrifices for what his kids might have done wrong (1:4–5), but is that why they died? Job's latter days *were* prosperous, but for the reason Bildad suggests? Job *was* pure and upright (8:6), but isn't that precisely why Satan attacked him?
- Rahab (9:13) is a mythological beast of the sea—symbolic of any great power; what else does Rahab represent in Psalm 87:4?

☐ **THURSDAY** | ## Zophar Speaks, Job Replies
Job 11–13

- Zophar has a high view of God (Job 11:7–9), but what's wrong with his belief about how God operates in a fallen world (11:13–20)?
- How is silence (Job 13:5) sometimes the wiser option (Proverbs 10:19; Ecclesiastes 5:1–7)? When did you last listen attentively to a hurting friend without making lots of comments?
- Job 13:15 is a famous phrase of trust in the midst of suffering; how did Jesus' final hours live out that truth?

☐ **FRIDAY** | ### Eliphaz Speaks, Job Replies
Job 14–17; Psalm 72

- Job 14:7–12 says that Job despairs of any afterlife; does that mean the Bible *teaches* there is no afterlife?
- Eliphaz is right in a general sense (Job 15:14–16), but why is applying that to explain Job's woes mistaken?
- In what sense is Job saying more than he knows in Job 16:19–21? (Compare 1 John 2:1; Hebrews 7:24–28.)

☐ **WEEKEND** | ### Bildad Speaks, Job Replies; Zophar Speaks, Job Replies
Job 18–21

- How do Bildad's words echo many well-meaning believers who erroneously think all problems stem from a bad relationship with God (Job 18:21)?
- What is the mood of Job 19:25–27? (Compare with Zechariah 14:3–4; 2 Corinthians 5:1–4; 1 John 3:2; Revelation 1:7.)
- Zophar's speech (Job 20) touches on the secondary theme of this book: the prosperity of the unrighteous. How does Job respond to that theme in Job 21:7, 9, 13–15, 30?
- Job disagrees with Zophar's belief that the wicked always get what they deserve; Job agrees that life *isn't* fair—but, like any sufferer, what does Job want (Job 21:19–20)?

THIS WEEK'S NOTES AND REFLECTIONS

_____

_____

_____

_____

_____

_____

_____

_____

_____

_____

_____

_____

OTC

Complete Track

JOB 22-42; PSALMS 73-75

MONDAY	Job 22-24; Psalm 73
TUESDAY	Job 25-28
WEDNESDAY	Job 29-31; Psalm 74
THURSDAY	Job 32-34
FRIDAY	Job 35-37; Psalm 75
WEEKEND	Job 38-42

Look for...
- Job's friends continuing to press him, in contrast to his maintaining his innocence
- Speech against Job by a fourth friend, the young man Elihu
- God's rebuke of all but vindication of Job
- Restoration of Job's fortunes

Activity
Pay attention to what people do to help those who suffer. What words are used? What actions are taken? What words and actions seem to truly help? What words and actions make the problem worse?

This Week's Prayer
Pray this prayer throughout the week: *"God, show me how to help those who suffer without sounding like Job's friends."*

☐ MONDAY | Eliphaz Speaks, Job Replies
Job 22–24; Psalm 73

- Job 22:4 is highly ironic; what has Satan seen in Job 2:3 that prompts these tests?
- Do you think Eliphaz's advice in 22:21 always brings the results he talks of (see 2 Timothy 3:12; Hebrews 11:36–39)?
- How does Job in Job 23:10 describe the benefits that trials can bring? (James in James 1:2–4 and Peter in 1 Peter 1:6–7 agree.)

☐ TUESDAY | Bildad Speaks, Job Replies
Job 25–28

- Bildad considers the "smallness" of humankind against the backdrop of God's glory in Job 25:6 and dwells on sin. The same wonder in Psalm 8:4–5 leads to a different emphasis. Which of these is your tendency?
- What hint of the afterlife do you see in Job 26:5?
- The poetic description of earth hanging unsupported in space (Job 26:7) is actually scientifically accurate.

☐ WEDNESDAY | Job Finishes His Lament
Job 29–31; Psalm 74

- Job 29:6 is a poetic description of abundance (see also Job 20:17; Deuteronomy 32:13–14; Numbers 13:27).
- Like Job in Job 30:20–23, we often falsely interpret God's silence as neglect and life's troubles as cruelty. God may choose to wait—which is not neglect—and he may allow hardships for higher purposes—which is not cruel (see Hebrews 12:5–11; Romans 8:38–39). How have you reacted recently to such experiences?
- Would it help you to copy Job's practice in Job 31:1 (see Matthew 5:28)?

☐ THURSDAY | Elihu Speaks
Job 32–34

- Elihu's message is that God uses suffering to train people (Job 33:29–30). This is true insight, but of what does Elihu unjustly accuse Job (34:8–11)?
- Elihu knows God is just and powerful (Job 34:12–15), therefore he can only conclude Job's suffering is warranted. But like Jesus' suffering (and sometimes ours), is suffering always "punishment"?

☐ **FRIDAY** | Elihu Continues
Job 35–37; Psalm 75

- Elihu is only partially right (Job 35:6–8); God is *complete* without us, but because he cares about us, how can our actions affect him (Zephaniah 3:17; Ephesians 4:30)?
- In Job 36:4, Elihu is either boasting about or mocking Job's confidence (27:5–6).
- Sometimes God uses identical circumstances for dual purposes (Job 37:13; Matthew 5:45); what effect should that have on our temptation to judge others?

☐ **WEEKEND** | God Speaks; Conclusion
Job 38–42

- In Job's circumstances, his friends presumed his guilt; Job presumed God's anger or injustice. Was either right (Job 38:2)?
- In Job 38–39, God calls Job and his friends to consider him and his glory. Ultimately, our pain must be absorbed in his wisdom, goodness, and power.
- A Leviathan (Job 41:1–34) is symbolic of great power; God's point is that he alone is more powerful than all other powers, real or imagined.
- Ultimately, a lover doesn't need answers. A lover needs the beloved to show up (Job 42:5–6). God shows up for Job—and for all of us someday (Revelation 21:3–4).
- What is the connection between God's blessing and our praying for others in Job 42:10?

THIS WEEK'S NOTES AND REFLECTIONS

_____
_____
_____
_____
_____
_____
_____
_____
_____
_____
_____

1 CHRONICLES; PSALMS 76-77

MONDAY	1 Chronicles 1-10; Psalm 76
TUESDAY	1 Chronicles 11-12
WEDNESDAY	1 Chronicles 13-15
THURSDAY	1 Chronicles 16-18; Psalm 77
FRIDAY	1 Chronicles 19-23
WEEKEND	1 Chronicles 24-29

Look for. . .

• Lots of names!
• Retelling of events from 1 and 2 Samuel, with spiritual commentary
• Prayer of Jabez
• Ark brought to Jerusalem
• Temple planned
• Solomon made king
• David's death

Activity

How many of your friends know their family history? How does knowing—or not knowing—your family's stories affect your daily life? What defining moments in your life would you like your family to remember?

This Week's Prayer

Pray this prayer throughout the week: *"God, help me take note of and pass on my life's lessons."*

☐ MONDAY | Genealogies R Us
1 Chronicles 1–10; Psalm 76

- We suggest you skim through these chapters; otherwise, you'll never make it through today's reading.
- Genealogies served God's people by reminding them of their heritage and God's faithfulness to his promise (Genesis 22:17–18); why might that be important to these post-captivity readers?
- Don't miss Jabez's famous prayer (1 Chronicles 4:9–10); make it your own today.

☐ TUESDAY | David's Leadership Established
1 Chronicles 11–12

- What does 1 Chronicles 11:9 highlight as the most important ingredient for successful leadership? What does verse 10 indicate is also important? Compare these two ingredients to Luke 2:52.
- Sadly, David betrayed one of the very "inner circle" who supported him (1 Chronicles 11:41; 2 Samuel 11).
- What is a tangible expression of appreciation you can show to a member of your "inner circle" today?

☐ WEDNESDAY | The Ark Brought to Jerusalem
1 Chronicles 13–15

- Is seeking human counsel contrary to listening for God (1 Chronicles 13:2; Proverbs 15:22)? What wise people are you listening to?
- Disobedience, even if well intentioned, is still wrong (1 Chronicles 13:9–10; Numbers 4:15; maybe God was gracious that *only* Uzzah died, considering Numbers 4:20; see also Acts 5:1–11). Did David learn his lesson (1 Chronicles 15:2, 12–13)?
- Michal apparently thought David's lack of kingly robes was beneath his position (1 Chronicles 15:29; 2 Samuel 6:20–23). How are you tempted to meet expectations of people who are important to you rather than resting in what God thinks of you?

☐ THURSDAY | Kingdom Promises
1 Chronicles 16–18; Psalm 77

- You'll encounter much of 1 Chronicles 16:8–36 again in Psalm 105. Why include it here? Israel needed to be reminded of her history as people returned from exile.
- Promises like 1 Chronicles 17:9–10 confused Jesus' followers, who thought he was going to fulfill them (Acts 1:6); how did he—and will he—do so (John 18:36; Daniel 2:44–45)?

☐ **FRIDAY** | David's Census; Preparation for the Temple
1 Chronicles 19–23

- First Chronicles 20:1–3 leaves out David's affair with Bathsheba (2 Samuel 11), an example of how biblical writers select material based on the purposes for their particular book (common in the Gospels).
- In 1 Chronicles 21:1, Satan urged David to take a census; 2 Samuel 24:1 says God urged him. How can both be true? (Hint: see a similar example of two wills at work in Genesis 50:19–20.)
- The site of Araunah's threshing floor (1 Chronicles 21:22; 22:1), which David bought from a non-Jew, became the foundation of the temple—a hint at God's inclusive heart.

☐ **WEEKEND** | Priests, Singers, Overseers; The Temple; David's Death
1 Chronicles 24–29

- Deadlock is sometimes resolved with "chance" means (1 Chronicles 24:5; Proverbs 18:18; Acts 1:26). Do you think this is a suitable method for decisions requiring wisdom and discernment?
- Musical instruments can be used in worship and prophesying (1 Chronicles 25:1); some priests even used accounting skills (1 Chronicles 26:20)!
- "Necessary" warfare did not exempt David from consequences (1 Chronicles 28:3).
- What "human-and-divine" plans (1 Chronicles 28:12) is God making through you?
- David set a fine leadership example (1 Chronicles 29:2–5), as did his lieutenants (29:6, 9); where do you need to "lead by example"?

THIS WEEK'S NOTES AND REFLECTIONS

2 CHRONICLES 1-18; PSALMS 78-80

MONDAY	2 Chronicles 1-3; Psalm 78
TUESDAY	2 Chronicles 4-5
WEDNESDAY	2 Chronicles 6-7; Psalm 79
THURSDAY	2 Chronicles 8-10
FRIDAY	2 Chronicles 11-13; Psalm 80
WEEKEND	2 Chronicles 14-18

Look for...

• Temple built and dedicated
• Solomon's prayer of dedication
• Queen of Sheba's visit
• Israel's rebellion against Rehoboam
• Good king Asa
• "Semi-" good king Jehoshaphat
• Ahab's rejection of God's word and his death

Activity

How many of your friends know their family history? How does knowing—or not knowing—your family's stories affect your daily life? What defining moments in your life would you like your family to remember?

This Week's Prayer

Pray this prayer throughout the week: *"God, help me take note of and pass on my life's lessons."*

☐ **MONDAY** | ## Solomon Starts the Temple
2 Chronicles 1–3; Psalm 78

- Solomon knew God treasured his people (2 Chronicles 1:10); are you a small group leader who should also pray this prayer (see also 1 Peter 5:2–4; Proverbs 8:12, 15–21)?
- Why a temple for God's *name* (2 Chronicles 2:1)? See verse 6 for a hint; also see 6:18–19.
- The temple site (2 Chronicles 3:1) is also where Abraham sacrificed Isaac (Genesis 22:2).
- Some of these very stones (2 Chronicles 3:3) can be seen today along the Western Wall. What did Jesus' disciples say about them in Mark 13:1–2?

☐ **TUESDAY** | ## Temple is Furnished
2 Chronicles 4–5

- God's words were physically placed at the center of his community (2 Chronicles 5:10). Where should they be spiritually placed now?
- No one knows what became of the manna and Aaron's rod (Exodus 16:32–34; Numbers 17:10–11; Hebrews 9:4).
- God's glory (2 Chronicles 5:13–14) was made visible. Where is that glory now? (See Hebrews 1:3; Luke 9:28–32; John 1:14; 17:20–22; 2 Corinthians 3:18; 2 Thessalonians 2:14.)

☐ **WEDNESDAY** | ## Temple is Dedicated
2 Chronicles 6–7; Psalm 79

- In his wonderful prayer (2 Chronicles 6:14–42), how do Solomon's words anticipate the worldwide, inclusive scope of God's plans (6: 32–33; see also Isaiah 56:6–8; Galatians 3:14, 26–29; Ephesians 3:6)?
- What similarities exist between 2 Chronicles 6:36 and Romans 3:23?
- Not following God exclusively cost Israel their homeland (2 Chronicles 7:21–22). What competes for *your* devotion these days?

☐ **THURSDAY** | ## Queen of Sheba; Rehoboam's Tyranny
2 Chronicles 8–10

- How is Solomon's interaction with the Queen of Sheba (2 Chronicles 9:1–8) an example of how we ought to interact and "live out" the gospel with unbelievers (Colossians 4:5–6; 1 Peter 2:12; 3:15)? When is the last time you did this?
- The prophecy spoken of in 2 Chronicles 10:15 is recorded in 1 Kings 11:29–39. How does this again illustrate the mystery of both human and divine responsibility in the unfolding of history?

☐ **FRIDAY** | ## Rehoboam's Fortifications; Shishak; Abijah
2 Chronicles 11–13; Psalm 80

- Never underestimate the power of a message from God (2 Chronicles 11:1–4). Is he telling *you* to keep speaking the truth somewhere?
- How does God sometimes use the consequences of sin to teach valuable lessons (2 Chronicles 12:8)?
- How do Numbers 18:19 and Leviticus 2:13 help explain the term "covenant of salt" in 2 Chronicles 13:5?
- How might salt, a preservative, symbolize aspects of God's covenant?

☐ **WEEKEND** | ## Asa and Jehoshaphat
2 Chronicles 14–18

- Just as marriage covenants can be renewed, so can covenants with God (2 Chronicles 15:12; Deuteronomy 29:1; Joshua 8:30–35; 24:19–27).
- What do 2 Chronicles 15:16; Matthew 10:37; and Psalm 27:10 say about putting loyalty to God above family?
- The first part of 2 Chronicles 16:9 has a timeless principle; how is *your* heart?
- The "Baals" (2 Chronicles 17:3) were some of several Canaanite gods; what form do idols come in our day?
- Jehoshaphat insisted on hearing from God (2 Chronicles 18:6). Yet once he heard his message, he apparently let the words "fall to the ground" (1 Samuel 3:19; 2 Chronicles 18:22, 28). What "fallen words" of God do you need to pick up and live out?

THIS WEEK'S NOTES AND REFLECTIONS

_____

_____

_____

_____

_____

_____

_____

_____

_____

_____

otc

Complete Track

2 CHRONICLES 19-36; PSALMS 81-84

MONDAY	2 Chronicles 19-21; Psalm 81
TUESDAY	2 Chronicles 22-24
WEDNESDAY	2 Chronicles 25-27; Psalm 82
THURSDAY	2 Chronicles 28-29; Psalm 83
FRIDAY	2 Chronicles 30-32; Psalm 84
WEEKEND	2 Chronicles 33-36

Look for. . .

- Jehoshaphat's battle won by prayer and praise
- God's protecting the line of David, fulfilling his promise
- Evil leaders dominating Judah's history
- Revivals led by good kings Hezekiah and Josiah
- Jerusalem finally falling to Nebuchadnezzar
- The land "resting" for seventy years, fulfilling prophecy

Activity

How many of your friends know their family history? How does knowing—or not knowing—your family's stories affect your daily life? What defining moments in your life would you like your family to remember?

This Week's Prayer

Pray this prayer throughout the week: *"God, help me take note of and pass on my life's lessons."*

☐ MONDAY | Jehoshaphat and Jehoram
2 Chronicles 19–21; Psalm 81

- Judges and other leaders were to exemplify God's character in their judgments (2 Chronicles 19:6–10); what about Christian leaders today (Matthew 18:18–19; 1 Peter 5:2–3)?
- Do you need to make Jehoshaphat's prayer yours (2 Chronicles 20:12)?
- An interesting battle strategy is described in 2 Chronicles 20:21–22; how is this like the first battle Israel fought in Joshua 6:20?
- What is the ultimate explanation for Israel's survival in 2 Chronicles 21:7?

☐ TUESDAY | Ahaziah, Athaliah, and Joash
2 Chronicles 22–24

- The temple was a safe haven for the child Joash (2 Chronicles 22:12) because Athaliah ignored spiritual matters and apparently never worshiped there.
- Read 2 Chronicles 23:16–17 for an important spiritual principle. In addition to turning *to* God, what must we turn *away* from (see also 2 Corinthians 10:5)?

☐ WEDNESDAY | Amaziah, Uzziah, and Jotham
2 Chronicles 25–27; Psalm 82

- Even though partially paid, the mercenaries were enraged, having been dismissed without plunder, the more significant source of income (2 Chronicles 25:10).
- How does Uzziah's life (2 Chronicles 26:16) illustrate the importance of finishing well—not just starting right (see also 1 Corinthians 9:24–27; 10:12; Proverbs 16:18)?
- What would help your "finish" be as strong as your "beginning"?

☐ THURSDAY | Wicked Ahaz, Good Hezekiah
2 Chronicles 28–29; Psalm 83

- "Father" (2 Chronicles 28:1) can obviously mean anyone earlier in the lineage, helpful to know when trying to decipher genealogies.
- How do Jesus and Paul compare with 2 Chronicles 28:14–15 in Luke 6:27, 31, 35; and Romans 12:20–21?
- What is the appeal of idolatry mentioned in 2 Chronicles 28:23?

☐ FRIDAY | Hezekiah's Reforms
2 Chronicles 30–32; Psalm 84

- Hezekiah's attempt at unity (2 Chronicles 30:1), some 250 years after the national split, is a testimony to the depth of his "revival."

- Doesn't *every* prayer (2 Chronicles 30:27) reach heaven? Yes, in the sense our omniscient God knows everything—but what *else* about prayer is taught in 1 Peter 3:7; 1 John 3:22; and Matthew 6:5–8?
- What was the sign of 2 Chronicles 32:24? (Read Isaiah 38:1–8.)

☐ **WEEKEND** | ## Manasseh and Josiah; Judah Falls Into Captivity
2 Chronicles 33–36

- Manasseh, one of Judah's worst kings (2 Chronicles 33:2–6, 9), was born during Hezekiah's fifteen-year life extension; maybe he should have just died!
- Manasseh's repentance and God's acceptance (2 Chronicles 33:13) is an amazing testimony to grace—grace that will also accept *you*.
- How does James 1:22–25 relate to 2 Chronicles 34:30–31?
- The pagan king Neco had more respect for God than Josiah did (2 Chronicles 35:21–22). Is it always obvious who's "in" and "out" in God's kingdom (1 Samuel 16:7; Matthew 7:21–23)?
- The seven-year cycle of Sabbath rest for the land (2 Chronicles 36:21; Leviticus 25:4) had been ignored for almost five hundred years; God provided them all at once during the Babylonian captivity (Leviticus 26:34–35; Jeremiah 29:10; Daniel 9:1–2). What spiritual principle might this illustrate?

THIS WEEK'S NOTES AND REFLECTIONS

_____

_____

_____

_____

_____

_____

_____

_____

_____

_____

_____

OTC

Complete Track

PROVERBS 1-15; PSALMS 85-88

MONDAY	Proverbs 1-2; Psalm 85
TUESDAY	Proverbs 3-4
WEDNESDAY	Proverbs 5-6; Psalm 86
THURSDAY	Proverbs 7-9; Psalm 87
FRIDAY	Proverbs 10-11; Psalm 88
WEEKEND	Proverbs 12-15

Look for...

- "The fear of the LORD is the beginning of wisdom"
- The benefits of wisdom, the cost of foolishness
- "Trust in the LORD with all your heart"
- The cost of infidelity
- Wisdom personified as a woman
- Rules for right living, speech, and spending

Activity

Did your family have any "wise sayings" that were often repeated or passed down? What are some of your favorite "quotes to live by" that don't come from the Bible? Over the coming weeks, make a collection of your own "words of wisdom" that have shaped your life.

This Week's Prayer

Pray this prayer throughout the week: *"God, give me wisdom from everyday life as well as learning truth from your Word."*

☐ **MONDAY** | ## Fear of the Lord, Benefits of Wisdom
Proverbs 1–2; Psalm 85

- Proverbs 1:1–7 lays the groundwork for the book; verse 7 is the cornerstone.
- How would you explain "fear of the LORD" in light of 1 John 4:18? (See also Psalm 112, especially the contrasting "fears" in verses 1 and 7–8.)
- Notice wisdom is a "she" in Proverbs 1:20; this book personifies wisdom (a literary device).
- According to Proverbs 1:20–21, how widely available is "wisdom"?

☐ **TUESDAY** | ## More Benefits of Wisdom
Proverbs 3–4

- How easy is Proverbs 3:4–5 for you to do?
- How do Malachi 3:10–12 and 2 Corinthians 9:6–11 illustrate Proverbs 3:9–10?
- How does Hebrews 12:5–6 use Proverbs 3:11–12?
- Your "heart" or inner self (Proverbs 4:23) is precious to God and needs to be precious to you. Is it?

☐ **WEDNESDAY** | ## Warnings Against Adultery
Proverbs 5–6; Psalm 86

- In addition to avoiding the act of immorality, what else should we do according to Proverbs 5:8?
- Proverbs 5:15–20 sounds much like the language of Song of Songs and encourages sexual delight—but exclusively with whom?
- Diligence never killed anyone (Proverbs 6:6–11), but what does laziness do?
- Adultery is always wrong (Exodus 20:14); according to Proverbs 6:32, what *else* is true of the person who commits it?

☐ **THURSDAY** | ## Anatomy of Seduction; Wisdom's Call
Proverbs 7–9; Psalm 87

- The phrase "apple of your eye" in Proverbs 7:2 (Deuteronomy 32:10; Zechariah 2:8) refers to the sensitive pupil. What's the application of this principle for your life?
- Proverbs 7 is a masterful description of the series of steps you have to take to "fall" into adultery; how many steps can you identify?
- Note the exaggeration "all at once" in Proverbs 7:22 when in fact this is a series of compromises.
- How readily available is wisdom according to Proverbs 8:4, 15–17?
- How lasting and life-giving are the pleasures of adultery according to Proverbs 9:17–18?

☐ **FRIDAY** | ## Power of the Tongue
Proverbs 10–11; Psalm 88

- Starting with chapter 10, Proverbs deals with wisdom applied in daily life. These are *general* principles, always subject to exceptions and special cases. In these chapters, the main themes are money—its use and misuse—and the power of the tongue for good or evil. What about *your* mouth lately?
- "Dishonest scales" in Proverbs 11:1 were used to cheat customers; are all your business dealings "his delight"?

☐ **WEEKEND** | ## Wise Choices; Upright and Wicked Contrasted
Proverbs 12–15

- Be kind to animals, says Proverbs 12:10; the person you are shows up *everywhere* eventually.
- What does Proverbs 12:15 say is needed to develop great wisdom (see also 9:9; 11:14; 13:20; and 15:22)? Who are you listening to these days?
- Wealth is not wrong, but what is the biblical method for gaining it as taught in Proverbs 12:11; 13:11? (And while your bank account grows, don't forget Proverbs 13:22; 11:24–25!)
- Why do you think the "way of death" in Proverbs 14:12 (see also 12:15 and 16:25) sometimes looks right?
- Failure isn't final for the wise; but what is needed for growth to come according to Proverbs 15:5, 10, 12, and 31–33?

THIS WEEK'S NOTES AND REFLECTIONS

OTC

PROVERBS 16–31; PSALMS 89–90

MONDAY	Proverbs 16–18
TUESDAY	Proverbs 19–20; Psalm 89
WEDNESDAY	Proverbs 21–22
THURSDAY	Proverbs 23–24
FRIDAY	Proverbs 25–26; Psalm 90
WEEKEND	Proverbs 27–31

Look for. . .

- Proverbs about the tongue, money, anger, the poor
- Descriptions of laziness
- Wise words from sources other than Solomon
- A wonderful picture of a godly woman

Activity

Did your family have any "wise sayings" that were often repeated or passed down? What are some of your favorite "quotes to live by" that don't come from the Bible? Over the coming weeks, make a collection of your own "words of wisdom" that have shaped your life.

This Week's Prayer

Pray this prayer throughout the week: *"God, give me wisdom from everyday life as well as learning truth from your Word."*

☐ MONDAY | Various Proverbs
Proverbs 16–18

- What does Paul say about Proverbs 16:4 in Romans 9:22–24?
- Many proverbs deal with words; what's the twist in Proverbs 17:28?
- What do wise people do in Proverbs 18:17 when someone says, "Let me tell you what *he* did to me!"?
- A bad marriage brings pain in Proverbs 17:1 (see also 1 Corinthians 7:32–35); what about a *good* one in Proverbs 18:22; 19:14; 31:10?

☐ TUESDAY | Various Proverbs
Proverbs 19–20; Psalm 89

- Proverbs 19:4, 6, like many proverbs, describes the irony of how things *are*, not how they ought to be.
- How does Jesus apply Proverbs 19:17 in Matthew 25:40?
- Do you think all substance abuse falls under the condemnation of Proverbs 20:1 and 21:17?
- Proverbs 20:5 is best done with a good, listening friend.
- How is Proverbs 20:27 similar to Romans 8:27 and 1 Corinthians 2:10–12, 16?

☐ WEDNESDAY | Various Proverbs; The Sayings of the Wise
Proverbs 21–22

- How is Proverbs 21:13 like Luke 6:38?
- Proverbs 21:30 (like Psalm 127:1) is true; why do some still try?
- How does Proverbs 22:3 apply to savings, retirement, and insurance?
- Proverbs 22:6 is often misunderstood as a promise that a believer's children won't stray. That misses the intent of Proverbs as *general* rules (not absolutes); after all, God, the perfect Father, "raised" Adam in the "way he should go"—yet look what he did!
- What is true of the lazy person's excuses in Proverbs 22:13?

☐ THURSDAY | More Sayings of the Wise
Proverbs 23–24

- What does Paul say about Proverbs 23:4–5 in 1 Timothy 6:9–10, 17?
- What signs of alcoholism can you identify in Proverbs 23:29–35?
- If God doesn't guarantee life without problems, what does Proverbs 24:16 mean?
- Many see Proverbs 24:27 as counsel to make provisions for a family before you start one.
- What does Jesus say about Proverbs 24:29 in Luke 6:27–28?
- What clues does laziness leave in Proverbs 24:30–34?

☐ **FRIDAY** | **More Proverbs of Solomon**
Proverbs 25–26; Psalm 90

- How does Jesus use Proverbs 25:7 in Luke 14:7–11?
- In what areas does Proverbs 25:16 and 17 advocate moderation?
- Based on Proverbs 25:20, what kind of encouragement does more harm than good (note also Romans 12:20)?
- Do Proverbs 26:4 and 5 contradict each other? The key is the word "according," used with slight differences in each verse (made clear by the second phrase of each verse).
- How does Peter use Proverbs 26:11 in 2 Peter 2:22?
- Read Proverbs 26:18–19: Are you a "teaser"—blind to the harm you do?

☐ **WEEKEND** | **More Proverbs of Solomon; Sayings of Agur and Lemuel**
Proverbs 27–31

- According to Proverbs 27:5–6, rebuke can be love, and some "nice" people may be *what*?
- Proverbs 27:17 is true, even when "sparks" result!
- How do James 5:16 and Psalm 32:3–5 expand on Proverbs 28:13?
- What does Proverbs 28:19 have to say about "get rich quick" schemes?
- Firm boundaries help kids according to Proverbs 29:15.
- Godly women can run businesses, serve their families, and teach with wisdom (Proverbs 31:10–31). Is your view of women's roles this big?

THIS WEEK'S NOTES AND REFLECTIONS

_____

_____

_____

_____

_____

_____

_____

_____

_____

OTC

Complete Track

ECCLESIASTES AND SONG OF SONGS; PSALMS 91-95

MONDAY	Ecclesiastes 1-3; Psalm 91
TUESDAY	Ecclesiastes 4-6; Psalm 92
WEDNESDAY	Ecclesiastes 7-8; Psalm 93
THURSDAY	Ecclesiastes 9-12
FRIDAY	Song of Songs 1-4; Psalm 94
WEEKEND	Song of Songs 5-8, Psalm 95

Look for...
- Meaninglessness of everything
- A time for everything
- The ability to enjoy life must come from God
- Life doesn't have the answers—but God does
- Love, sex, and romance as gifts from God

Activity
Did your family have any "wise sayings" that were often repeated or passed down? What are some of your favorite "quotes to live by" that don't come from the Bible? Over the coming weeks, make a collection of your own "words of wisdom" that have shaped your life.

This Week's Prayer
Pray this prayer throughout the week: *"God, give me wisdom from everyday life as well as learning truth from your Word."*

☐ **MONDAY** | ## All is Meaningless Under the Sun
Ecclesiastes 1–3; Psalm 91

- Ecclesiastes 1:1, 12, 16 point to Solomon as the author, but that isn't known for certain.
- Ecclesiastes 2:24–25 and 3:12–15 are the key verses in this whole book. If life "under the sun" doesn't make sense, what do we need in order to find satisfaction?
- We yearn for "eternity" (Ecclesiastes 3:11); how is that a clue as to why life "under the sun" (noneternal) is so wearisome?

☐ **TUESDAY** | ## God is Needed to Enjoy Life's Blessings
Ecclesiastes 4–6; Psalm 92

- If Ecclesiastes 4:9–12 is used at a wedding, what's the "third strand"?
- What clue is in Ecclesiastes 5:7 for how to make sense of this meaningless life "under the sun"?
- Ecclesiastes 5:10–17 is a splash of cold water to anyone foolish enough to make material pursuits their life's goal; what truth in 5:19–20 provides the missing ingredient for ultimate satisfaction?

☐ **WEDNESDAY** | ## Life Under the Sun is Unfair
Ecclesiastes 7–8; Psalm 93

- Why can a funeral—though a sad experience—teach us more about the meaning of life than a party (Ecclesiastes 7:2–4)?
- Ecclesiastes 7:6 contains a rhyming wordplay in Hebrew, something like "nettles under kettles."
- Does God always bless the righteous and punish the wicked according to Ecclesiastes 7:15; 8:14?
- How is Ecclesiastes 7:29 a great summary of Genesis 1–3?

☐ **THURSDAY** | ## More Wisdom and Warnings; Remember Your Creator
Ecclesiastes 9–12

- How do Colossians 3:23–24 and John 9:4 reinterpret Ecclesiastes 9:10 in light of eternal rewards?
- Although nobody "under the sun" remembered the man in Ecclesiastes 9:15, what about 1 Corinthians 15:58; Matthew 6:4; 10:42?
- Is Ecclesiastes 10:19 a promise—or irony?
- Ecclesiastes 12:1–7 is a poetic description of a body aging and dying.
- If nails are reliable places to hang things, what's the meaning of Ecclesiastes 12:11?
- How does Ecclesiastes summarize its entire message in 12:13–14?

☐ FRIDAY | Lovers' Anticipation
Song of Songs 1–4; Psalm 94

- Song of Songs is an unabashed celebration of marital love; how does 1:2 set the tone for what's to come?
- Song of Songs 2:7 (also 3:5; 8:4) is an admonition about not rushing sexual intimacy; is that a message you need to hear?
- "Solomon" (Song of Songs 3:7–11) may be metaphorical, the groom being "kingly" in her sight (in Song of Songs 1:7 he's a shepherd).
- Why should "sister" (Song of Songs 4:9) be understood as an intimate relationship, not a literal sibling (compare with "friend" in 5:16)?

☐ WEEKEND | Lovers Revel in Each Other
Song of Songs 5–8, Psalm 95

- These descriptions (Song of Songs 4:1–7; 5:10–16; 6:4–9) sound strange to our ears, but what do you know about that culture that would cause listeners to consider them beautiful?
- "Wall" and "door" (Song of Songs 8:9–10) may refer to opposites: *guarded purity* and *moral laxity*. What's the writer saying about those two conditions?

THIS WEEK'S NOTES AND REFLECTIONS

_____
_____
_____
_____
_____
_____
_____
_____
_____
_____
_____
_____
_____

OTC

Complete Track

MONDAY	Isaiah 1-2; Psalm 96
TUESDAY	Isaiah 3-5; Psalm 97
WEDNESDAY	Isaiah 6-8; Psalm 98
THURSDAY	Isaiah 9-11; Psalm 99
FRIDAY	Isaiah 12-15; Psalm 100
WEEKEND	Isaiah 16-22;, Psalm 101

Look for. . .

- Sins red as scarlet becoming white as snow
- A holy God presiding over the affairs of humankind
- Immanuel—"God with us"—prophesied
- Wonderful Counselor . . . Prince of Peace
- Coming of the Branch—another term for Messiah
- Pagan nations as well as Judah warned of judgment
- Babylon's fall parallel to Satan's fall

Activity

Generally we prefer encouraging words to corrective ones. But both are necessary. During the coming weeks, notice all the messages around you designed to warn or rebuke: at home, the office, school, newspapers, TV, Internet, and so on. Which ones seem effective? Which don't get heard? What makes you more receptive—or defensive?

This Week's Prayer

Pray this prayer throughout the week: *"God, open me up to correction—whenever needed, from whomever you send."*

☐ MONDAY | God's Response to a Nation's Sin
Isaiah 1–2; Psalm 96

- Judah was very "religious"; so why is God angry (Isaiah 1:11–17)?
- God's offer in Isaiah 1:18 is valid for all times—for *you!* How do forgiven people live according to verse 19?
- What parallels can you make to Judah's sins in Isaiah 2:6–8 and people in our day?

☐ TUESDAY | God's Judgment; Song of the Vineyard
Isaiah 3–5; Psalm 97

- "Children" (Isaiah 3:4) is meant literally (2 Kings 21:1), but how is it also symbolic (2 Kings 23:36–37; 24:8–9, 18–19)?
- The Branch (Isaiah 4:2; 11:1–5) is Messiah. The mission described here began with Jesus' first coming; when will it culminate (Hebrews 9:28; 2 Thessalonians 1:6–10)?
- How do the six "woes" of Isaiah 5:8–23 compare with the sins of our society?

☐ WEDNESDAY | Holy, Holy, Holy; Immanuel
Isaiah 6–8; Psalm 98

- Despite bad political news (Isaiah 6:1; 2 Chronicles 26), Isaiah saw God enthroned in power. Is that still true when hard news reaches us today?
- How did Jesus use Isaiah 6:9–10 in Matthew 13:13–15?
- Immanuel (meaning "God with us," Isaiah 7:14; 8:8) first signified a temporary deliverance from Rezin and Aram (Isaiah 7:16); in Jesus, we have permanent deliverance from sin (Matthew 1:23).
- Desperate people turn to the occult (Isaiah 8:19–22) rather than Scripture (v. 20). Why is that still a temptation in our day?

☐ THURSDAY | A Child is Born; The Branch
Isaiah 9–11; Psalm 99

- From Galilee comes a "great light" (Isaiah 9:1–2) who is more than human (9:6–7): Messiah Jesus. How did the Pharisees miss—or reject—this verse in John 7:52?
- Civil actions (Isaiah 10:1–4) betray our inner condition; what do yours say about you?
- The Branch (Isaiah 11:1), the Root of Jesse (11:10), is none other than Jesus (Jeremiah 23:5; 33:15; Zechariah 3:8–9, 6:12–13), who will someday bring peace everywhere (Isaiah 11:6–9).

☐ **FRIDAY** | Songs of Deliverance; Prophecies Against the Nations
Isaiah 12–15; Psalm 100

- God, who condemns, is also the one who graciously saves (Isaiah 12:1–2); how have you experienced both of these aspects from him?
- God's judgment of pagan nations (Isaiah 13–21) teaches that God holds the whole world accountable to him, obedience is blessed, and disobedience is ultimately punished.
- In Babylon's fall (Isaiah 14:12–15; also King of Tyre in Ezekiel 28:12–17), many see a parallel to Satan's fall.

☐ **WEEKEND** | Oracles to Many Nations; More Judgment to Come
Isaiah 16–22; Psalm 101

- God offers hope that Messiah will help Moab (Isaiah 16:5), not just Judah and Israel. What does this reveal about God's heart?
- Isaiah 19:18–25 predicts these pagan nations will turn to the Lord. How is this fulfilled today as Israel's God is being worshiped in Christian churches?
- "Valley of Vision" (Isaiah 22:1) refers to Jerusalem, either sarcastically (since Jerusalem is on a hill) or literally to a place nearby the city where Isaiah had this vision.
- How is Isaiah 22:13 used by Jesus in Luke 12:18–20 and by Paul in 1 Corinthians 15:32?
- Isaiah's many warnings do two things: They urge individuals to repent (though unfortunately the nations don't), and they confirm God is at work when predicted events come to pass. Which of these reminders do you most need today?

THIS WEEK'S NOTES AND REFLECTIONS

_____

_____

_____

_____

_____

_____

_____

_____

_____

_____

Complete Track

ISAIAH 23-44; PSALMS 102-103

MONDAY	Isaiah 23-26
TUESDAY	Isaiah 27-29; Psalm 102
WEDNESDAY	Isaiah 30-32
THURSDAY	Isaiah 33-36
FRIDAY	Isaiah 37-39; Psalm 103
WEEKEND	Isaiah 40-44

Look for. . .

• The end—and rebuilding—of the world

• Trust in Egypt condemned

• History of Hezekiah

• God's comforting of his people with promise of renewal

• "I am He"

• Condemnation of idolatry

Activity

Generally we prefer encouraging words to corrective ones. But both are necessary. During the coming weeks, notice all the messages around you designed to warn or rebuke: at home, the office, school, newspapers, TV, Internet, and so on. Which ones seem effective? Which don't get heard? What makes you more receptive—or defensive?

This Week's Prayer

Pray this prayer throughout the week: *"God, open me up to correction— whenever needed, from whomever you send."*

☐ **MONDAY** | ## World Judgment
Isaiah 23–26

- Tyre (Isaiah 23) was destroyed by the Babylonians; centuries later, Alexander the Great finished off the island fortress by building a bridge to it with rubble from the mainland city (Ezekiel 26:12).
- What other New Testament book sounds like the worldwide judgments predicted in chapters 24–27?
- Even in times of turmoil and judgment, Isaiah 26:3 is true; how do Philippians 4:7 and John 14:27 underscore this reality?

☐ **TUESDAY** | ## Ephraim and Jerusalem
Isaiah 27–29; Psalm 102

- God defeats the mythological Leviathan (Isaiah 27:1); how would that paint a picture to people in that day of his total reign and superiority?
- Isaiah 28:10 in Hebrew sounds like the babble of children; Isaiah is quoting what those mocking him say about him.
- What parallels can you make between how the foreign Assyrians would teach Israel to repent in Isaiah 28:11 and how the foreign language of tongues—the work of the Spirit—teaches Israel to turn to Messiah in 1 Corinthians 14:18–22?
- How does 1 Peter 2:6–7 interpret Isaiah 28:16?
- How did Jesus use Isaiah 29:13 in Matthew 15:8–9 and Mark 7:6–7?

☐ **WEDNESDAY** | ## Trust in Egypt Condemned
Isaiah 30–32

- How were Israel's alliances (Isaiah 30:1–2; 31:1; 2 Kings 18:21) a spiritual, not just political, problem?
- According to the following verses, why do you think people in rebellion prefer lies: Isaiah 30:10–11; John 3:19–20; Romans 1:18, 21–22; 2 Thessalonians 2:10–11?
- How can you take to heart the truth of Isaiah 30:18 today?
- Why will Isaiah 32:1–8 only occur with Christ's reign?

☐ **THURSDAY** | ## Distress and Help; The Coming Eternal Kingdom
Isaiah 33–36

- If God is the fire (Isaiah 33:14) that burns away impurities, what happens if we choose to cling to sin (Hebrews 12:29)?
- Is "day" and "year" (Isaiah 34:8) a literal length of time (2 Peter 3:10; 1 Thessalonians 5:2)?
- Someday Messiah will bring the kingdom mentioned in Isaiah 35:5–10 in fullness.
- Chapters 36–39 are historical, parallel to 2 Kings 18–20.

☐ **FRIDAY** | ## Hezekiah
Isaiah 37–39; Psalm 103

- How is Hezekiah's prayer in Isaiah 37:14–20 a great example for us?
- Hezekiah's pride (Isaiah 39:2) led to judgment (39:6–7); his reaction (Isaiah 39:8) may mean that he was relieved or that he thought it appropriate.

☐ **WEEKEND** | ## Comfort; I am He; Idolatry Ridiculed
Isaiah 40–44

- John the Baptist saw himself fulfilling Isaiah 40:3 (Mark 1:2–4).
- Can we still count on the promise of Isaiah 40:8 today (Isaiah 55:11; Jeremiah 23:29; Matthew 24:35)?
- The "servant" (Isaiah 42:1) is Israel (Isaiah 41:8; 44:1), but the "Servant" *par excellence* is Jesus; how do God's words in Matthew 3:17 echo Isaiah 41:8?
- You, too, are redeemed (Isaiah 43:1) and precious to him (Isaiah 43:4). Do you believe this? What difference will it make today?
- God's "I am he" (Isaiah 41:4; 43:10, 13, 25; 46:4; 48:12) is repeated by Jesus (Mark 13:6; John 8:56–58; 13:19; 18:6); what mere man would say that?
- "First and last" (Isaiah 44:6) is applied to Jesus in Revelation 1:17–18; how many "firsts and lasts" can there be?

THIS WEEK'S NOTES AND REFLECTIONS

_____

_____

_____

_____

_____

_____

_____

_____

_____

_____

_____

_____

OTC

Complete Track

MONDAY	Isaiah 45-47
TUESDAY	Isaiah 48-50; Psalm 104
WEDNESDAY	Isaiah 51-53
THURSDAY	Isaiah 54-57
FRIDAY	Isaiah 58-60; Psalm 105
WEEKEND	Isaiah 61-66

Look for...

- Cyrus, a pagan "messiah" used by God to bring judgment
- The prediction of the Suffering Servant
- God to judge and remake the world
- The final triumph of God's universal kingdom

Activity

Generally we prefer encouraging words to corrective ones. But both are necessary. During the coming weeks, notice all the messages around you designed to warn or rebuke: at home, the office, school, newspapers, TV, Internet, and so on. Which ones seem effective? Which don't get heard? What makes you more receptive—or defensive?

This Week's Prayer

Pray this prayer throughout the week: *"God, open me up to correction— whenever needed, from whomever you send."*

☐ MONDAY | Cyrus; Babylon Rebuked
Isaiah 45–47

- Cyrus is God's "anointed" (Isaiah 45:1) or "messiah" (that word means "anointed one"), chosen to free captives to rebuild Jerusalem.
- How was the potter/clay comparison in Isaiah 45:9 also used by Jeremiah (Jeremiah 18:1–10) and Paul (Romans 9:20)?
- Who is Jesus according to Isaiah 45:22–24 and Philippians 2:10–11?
- Are you planing to consult astrologers or fortune-tellers (Isaiah 47:10–15; note sarcasm in v. 12)? *Don't!*

☐ TUESDAY | Stubborn Israel; Freedom and the Servant
Isaiah 48–50; Psalm 104

- What comparison can you make between God's leading his people out of Egypt to the Promised Land at the time of the Exodus and his leading them home from captivity in Babylon (Isaiah 48:20–22)?
- Israel's restoration includes non-Jews (Isaiah 49:6). How does this help fulfill Genesis 12:3? How does the church "complete" this plan (see Romans 11:25–27)?
- How are Isaiah 49:15–16 and 50:6 hauntingly echoed in the crucifixion of Jesus?

☐ WEDNESDAY | Suffering Servant
Isaiah 51–53

- How does Paul agree with Isaiah 52:7 in Romans 10:15 (and note how he quotes Isaiah 53:1 in Romans 10:16; see also John 12:37–41)? What "good news" or "message" is Paul talking about?
- The extent of Isaiah 52:10 is no exaggeration; how is the church taking the message of salvation "to the ends of the earth" in our day?
- Isaiah 53 is one of the most amazing chapters in the whole Old Testament, accurately predicting Jesus' death (vs. 4–8), burial (v. 9), resurrection (vs. 10–11), and atonement (vs. 4–6, 11–12).

☐ THURSDAY | Future Glory; Open Invitation to the Contrite
Isaiah 54–57

- What parallels can you make between Israel's chastisement and restoration in Isaiah 54 and ours as believers in Hebrews 12:5–11?
- How is Luke 21:15 an application of Isaiah 54:17?
- How does Isaiah 55:10–11 compare with Hebrews 4:12–13?
- Our God loves to find lost sheep (Isaiah 56:8)!

- What is the significance of "inheriting the land" in Isaiah 57:13; Psalm 37:11; and Matthew 5:5?
- How does Isaiah 57:21 compare with Philippians 4:7?

☐ **FRIDAY** | **True Fasting; Glory to Come**
Isaiah 58–60; Psalm 105

- Are spiritual practices substitutes for compassion (Isaiah 58:6–7; see also James 2:15–17)?
- What is the common principle in Isaiah 59:1–2; Psalm 66:18; Proverbs 28:9; and 1 Peter 3:7?
- Isaiah 60:1–2 is the same light of Matthew 5:14, brought about by the light of John 9:5.
- How does Isaiah 60:19 compare with Revelation 21:23?

☐ **WEEKEND** | **Year of Lord's Favor; New Heavens and New Earth**
Isaiah 61–66

- Jesus began his ministry quoting Isaiah 61:1–2 (Luke 4:16–19); how will his second coming fulfill the second part of Isaiah 61:2 (Revelation 19:11–15)?
- How does Paul paraphrase Isaiah 64:4–5 in 1 Corinthians 2:9?
- Why are "righteous acts" filthy (Isaiah 64:6) in God's sight?
- Who is the "seeker" in Isaiah 65:1 (1 John 4:19; Romans 10:20–21)?
- How does Jesus use Isaiah 66:1 in Matthew 5:34–35?

THIS WEEK'S NOTES AND REFLECTIONS

_____
_____
_____
_____
_____
_____
_____
_____
_____

Complete Track

PSALMS 106-107

Catch-Up Week

This week is a catch-up week. If you have fallen behind in the reading, use this time to get caught up. If you're on track, read whatever you like—and enjoy the break! Either way, the only additional assignment this week is to read Psalms 106–107.

Next week, you'll resume your regular daily reading schedule.

JEREMIAH 1–20; PSALMS 108–109

MONDAY	Jeremiah 1–3
TUESDAY	Jeremiah 4–5; Psalm 108
WEDNESDAY	Jeremiah 6–8
THURSDAY	Jeremiah 9–11
FRIDAY	Jeremiah 12–14; Psalm 109
WEEKEND	Jeremiah 15–20

Look for...
- The young prophet called into service
- "Circumcise your heart"
- Idolatry condemned
- Pictures of utter destruction to come
- False prophets to be judged
- Lessons in the potter's house

Activity
Generally we prefer encouraging words to corrective ones. But both are necessary. During the coming weeks, notice all the messages around you designed to warn or rebuke: at home, the office, school, newspapers, TV, Internet, and so on. Which ones seem effective? Which don't get heard? What makes you more receptive—or defensive?

This Week's Prayer
Pray this prayer throughout the week: *"God, open me up to correction— whenever needed, from whomever you send."*

☐ MONDAY | Jeremiah's Call
Jeremiah 1–3

- How does Jeremiah 1:6–7 compare with 1 Timothy 4:12?
- In Hebrew, God uses a pun in Jeremiah 1:11–12 (see NIV text note).
- The twofold sin of Israel was to abandon God and then try to meet their spiritual thirst on their own (Jeremiah 2:13); God didn't mind them being thirsty but knew false religion never satisfies. What "cisterns" are you digging?
- How is Jeremiah 2:25 the cry of every addict?

☐ TUESDAY | Self-Deception
Jeremiah 4–5; Psalm 108

- How is "heart circumcision" (Jeremiah 4:4) described in Romans 2:28–29; Colossians 2:11; and Deuteronomy 30:6?
- In Jeremiah 5:12–13, the people lie about God; what truths are they denying (see also Jeremiah 5:21–25)?
- Jeremiah 5:31 says people sometimes actually prefer to be spiritually misled (see 2 Timothy 4:3–4). Do you?

☐ WEDNESDAY | False Religion Condemned
Jeremiah 6–8

- When sin is serious, do you downplay the consequences (Jeremiah 6:14–15; cf. Isaiah 57:21)?
- As the "tester of metals" (Jeremiah 6:27–30), Jeremiah concludes that Judah was too impure; dross-filled metal—and people—are rejected.
- The temple (Jeremiah 7:4, 9–11) had become a fetish, and the people thought hiding out there would protect them; how does Jesus quote Jeremiah 7:11 in Matthew 21:13?
- "Queen of Heaven" (Jeremiah 7:18) was a popular ancient fertility goddess.

☐ THURSDAY | Idolatry Condemned; Broken Covenant
Jeremiah 9–11

- Chapter 9 continues the lament begun in Jeremiah 8:18 (remember, chapter divisions came much later).
- How is Jeremiah 9:23–24 a classic statement of the heart of true spirituality?
- Jeremiah 10:3–4 is not a Christmas tree, as some falsely allege, but an idol.
- Jeremiah wants the punishers punished (Jeremiah 10:25; also 11:20); how is this cry for justice consistent with God's heart?

☐ **FRIDAY** | ## The Linen Belt; False Prophets
Jeremiah 12–14; Psalm 109

- Jeremiah asks God about his delays (Jeremiah 12:1–4); what does God tell Jeremiah to do (12:5–6)?
- The linen belt (Jeremiah 13:1–11) pictured Judah's original purity—but what is its current condition?
- What kind of prophet would tell sinners that no harm will befall them (Jeremiah 14:13)? A *false* prophet (see Matthew 7:22–23)!

☐ **WEEKEND** | ## Disaster Coming; Sinful Hearts; At the Potter's House
Jeremiah 15–20

- Moses and Samuel (Jeremiah 15:1) were great intercessors, but Judah's sin was so great that the prayers of these two men wouldn't help.
- How does Jeremiah 17:8 compare with Psalm 1:3?
- Jeremiah 17:9 is true of our sinful heart; what does God gives us instead (Ezekiel 36:26–27)?
- Clay needs to be soft in order to be reshaped; what kind of clay is Judah according to Jeremiah 18:11–15? What kind of clay are you?
- What do you learn about Jeremiah through his prayer in 20:7–18?

THIS WEEK'S NOTES AND REFLECTIONS

_____

_____

_____

_____

_____

_____

_____

_____

_____

_____

_____

Complete Track

JEREMIAH 21-46; PSALMS 110-114

MONDAY	Jeremiah 21-23; Psalm 110
TUESDAY	Jeremiah 24-27; Psalm 111
WEDNESDAY	Jeremiah 28-30; Psalm 112
THURSDAY	Jeremiah 31-32; Psalm 113
FRIDAY	Jeremiah 33-36; Psalm 114
WEEKEND	Jeremiah 37-46

Look for...
- Seventy years of captivity prophesied
- False prophets giving false assurances
- The new covenant
- Jeremiah's scroll rejected and burned
- Jeremiah "in the pits"
- False religion condemned
- Jeremiah's ministry in Egypt

Activity
Generally we prefer encouraging words to corrective ones. But both are necessary. During the coming weeks, notice all the messages around you designed to warn or rebuke: at home, the office, school, newspapers, TV, Internet, and so on. Which ones seem effective? Which don't get heard? What makes you more receptive—or defensive?

This Week's Prayer
Pray this prayer throughout the week: *"God, open me up to correction—whenever needed, from whomever you send."*

☐ **MONDAY** | ## Evil Kings and Lying Prophets Condemned
Jeremiah 21–23; Psalm 110

- Why does God fight his own people in Jeremiah 21:5–7? What's the way out in 21:8–9?
- What timeless leadership principles can you see in Jeremiah 22:13–17?
- Jeremiah 23:5–6 is about Messiah, Jesus, but complete fulfillment awaits his second coming.
- What kind of dreams and prophecies *aren't* from God according to Jeremiah 23:25–40 (see also Deuteronomy 13:1–4; Lamentations 2:14; and Colossians 2:18)?

☐ **TUESDAY** | ## Seventy Years Captivity; Jeremiah Threatened
Jeremiah 24–27; Psalm 111

- What fulfilled prophecy in Jeremiah 25:11–12 (see 2 Chronicles 36:21) is another example of why we can trust God's Word?
- Are you prepared to follow God even when opposed (Jeremiah 16:11)? What opposition do you face today?
- How is God's using evil Nebechadnezzar (Jeremiah 27:6–7) similar to his using Judas's choices (Acts 1:16)?

☐ **WEDNESDAY** | ## Another False Prophet; Restoration to Come
Jeremiah 28–30; Psalm 112

- The message of Hananiah (Jeremiah 28:2–4) was more welcome than Jeremiah's— though not from God—and he ultimately paid for his false claims (28:15–17). What "message" in your life sounds good right now, but isn't from God?
- What timeless principles can you take to heart from Jeremiah 29:11–13?
- Where can God find such leaders as in Jeremiah 30:21, and such people as in 30:22, today? In *you?*

☐ **THURSDAY** | ## New Covenant
Jeremiah 31–32; Psalm 113

- At the time of Jesus' birth (Matthew 2:18), Herod's massacre caused a similar weeping as is recorded Jeremiah 31:15, which Matthew saw as a "filling out"—or "fulfillment"—of this passage.
- The new covenant (or "testament") of Jeremiah 31:31–34 was inaugurated by Jesus (Hebrews 8:8–12; 10:16–17); how much of it has happened for you?
- Though Jeremiah 32:27 is true, ironically God *wasn't* going to use that power to defeat Israel's pagan enemies at that time. How do verses 37–41 give hope?

☐ **FRIDAY** | ## Restoration; Recabites; Scroll Burned
Jeremiah 33–36; Psalm 114

- In what sense has Christ and the church fulfilled Jeremiah 33:17–22 (see Hebrews 10:10–18)?
- The Recabites weren't full-blooded Jews but understood the importance of obedience (Jeremiah 35:14, 16); how is that fact a stinging rebuke (Romans 2:17–27)?
- Repentance is shown by tearing one's clothes and sitting in ashes; what then is the irony of Jehoiakim's actions in Jeremiah 36:23–24?

☐ **WEEKEND** | ## Jeremiah Imprisoned; Jerusalem Falls; Flight to Egypt
Jeremiah 37–46

- From one pit (Jeremiah 37:16) to another (38:6), things go from bad to worse, but Jeremiah stays true to God and his Word. Will you do the same?
- What clue is in Jeremiah 42:17 concerning the hypocrisy of Jeremiah 42:5–6?
- Is true religion always proved by "prosperity" and "answered prayer" (see Jeremiah 44:17–18)?
- What additional blame-shifting is behind the women's words in Jeremiah 44:19?

THIS WEEK'S NOTES AND REFLECTIONS

_____

_____

_____

_____

_____

_____

_____

_____

_____

_____

_____

_____

_____

OTC

Complete Track

JEREMIAH 47–52; LAMENTATIONS; EZEKIEL 1–8; PSALMS 115–118

MONDAY	Jeremiah 47–48; Psalm 115
TUESDAY	Jeremiah 49–50; Psalm 116
WEDNESDAY	Jeremiah 51–52; Psalm 117
THURSDAY	Lamentations 1–3; Psalm 118
FRIDAY	Lamentations 4–5; Ezekiel 1
WEEKEND	Ezekiel 2–8

Look for...
- Jeremiah, the "weeping prophet"
- Babylon to be judged
- Jerusalem's fall
- God's compassions never failing, they're new every morning
- Ezekiel's bizarre visions
- Ezekiel's acting out lessons from God

Activity
Generally we prefer encouraging words to corrective ones. But both are necessary. During the coming weeks, notice all the messages around you designed to warn or rebuke: at home, the office, school, newspapers, TV, Internet, and so on. Which ones seem effective? Which don't get heard? What makes you more receptive—or defensive?

This Week's Prayer
Pray this prayer throughout the week: *"God, open me up to correction— whenever needed, from whomever you send."*

☐ MONDAY | Philistines and Moab Judged
Jeremiah 47–48; Psalm 115

- History tells us the Philistines were captured and deported, just as predicted in Jeremiah 47:4. But unlike Israel, they were never restored to their land.
- Can you see why Jeremiah has been called "the weeping prophet" (Jeremiah 48:31–32)?

☐ TUESDAY | Israel's Neighbors Judged; Fall of Babylon
Jeremiah 49–50; Psalm 116

- The restoration of the Ammonites and Elamites (Jeremiah 49:6, 39) and Moabites (48:47) is not described in detail, but note how God includes even pagan nations in his blessings. What would be a modern-day application of this principle?
- Bel and Marduk (Jeremiah 50:2) are Babylonian gods who will be seen as powerless once God acts. Who would have believed Jeremiah when Babylon was the world's greatest superpower? What promises of God seem "impossible" to you right now?
- How is guilt removed: by God's grace or human effort (Jeremiah 50:20)?

☐ WEDNESDAY | Babylon Repaid; Fall of Jerusalem Recounted
Jeremiah 51–52; Psalm 117

- Why would God "swear by himself" (Jeremiah 51:14; see Hebrews 6:13–17)?
- What is the spiritual parallel to "leaving Babylon" (Jeremiah 51:6, 45) in Revelation 18:4?
- Chapter 52 repeats and expands information from Jeremiah 39:1–10 (and 2 Kings 25), possibly as a literary device or as a historic appendix.

☐ THURSDAY | God's Faithfulness Even in Times of Distress
Lamentations 1–3; Psalm 118

- Though Jeremiah knew judgment was coming, Jerusalem's fall prompted this poetic lament (Lamentations 1:1).
- What is the "footstool" (Lamentations 2:1, 7) that God no longer remembered (2 Chronicles 28:2)?
- God's "new morning mercies" (Lamentations 3:22–23) are all the more remarkable, coming as they do to Jeremiah—and to us—in the midst of great woes. What "new mercies" do you need from him today?

☐ **FRIDAY** | **Restore Us; Ezekiel's Vision**
Lamentations 4–5; Ezekiel 1

- How is it possible to both feel despair (Lamentations 4:11, 16) at God's actions, and yet call on him for help (Lamentations 5:1; see also 5:19–22)? Hint: look in the mirror!
- Rather than try to decipher the details of Ezekiel's vision (Ezekiel 1:4–28), it's best to stick with the main point: God got Ezekiel's attention and assured him he was there, in Babylon, in all his glory (1:28).

☐ **WEEKEND** | **Ezekiel's Call; Parables; Idolatry in the Temple**
Ezekiel 2–8

- "Son of man" (Ezekiel 2:1) emphasizes Ezekiel's humanity and dependence on God.
- How might Ezekiel 2:4–7 apply today?
- What warnings might God be giving you to share with others (Ezekiel 3:17)?
- How does Luke 12:47–48 help explain the severity of God in Ezekiel 5:5–9?
- God keeps his promises—including promises of judgment (Ezekiel 6:10).
- Why do you suppose God won't answer in Ezekiel 7:26 and 8:18? (Hint: see Isaiah 59:2.)

THIS WEEK'S NOTES AND REFLECTIONS

Complete Track

EZEKIEL 9–34; PSALM 119

MONDAY	Ezekiel 9–13
TUESDAY	Ezekiel 14–16; Psalm 119:1–64
WEDNESDAY	Ezekiel 17–19
THURSDAY	Ezekiel 20–22; Psalm 119:65–120
FRIDAY	Ezekiel 23–26; Psalm 119:121–176
WEEKEND	Ezekiel 27–34

Look for. . .

- The longest chapter in the Bible (Psalm 119)
- God's glory leaving the temple
- Israel/Judah compared to unfaithful spouses
- Personal responsibility for sin stressed
- Ezekiel, a watchman, sent to warn
- Unfaithful shepherds/leaders rebuked

Activity

God used pivotal experiences in Israel's history to shape their identity: the exodus from Egypt, the conquest of Canaan, and the exile in Babylon, to name a few. Similarly, we all have defining moments in our own lives that determine the path we take. In the next few weeks, reflect on what those have been in your life. What resulting resolves have you made—what "stakes in the ground" have you driven—because of those pivotal experiences?

This Week's Prayer

Pray this prayer throughout the week: *"God, open my eyes to my defining moments and help me live the mission that flows out of them."*

☐ **MONDAY** | God's Glory Departs; God Our Sanctuary
Ezekiel 9–13

- The glory of the Lord departs from the temple: first to the door (Ezekiel 9:3), then to the cherubim (10:18), then to the east gate (10:19), then to the Mount of Olives outside Jerusalem (11:23). Why (see 1 Kings 9:6–9)?
- Where is the true sanctuary (see Ezekiel 11:16)?
- How is Ezekiel 11:19 like the new birth of John 3:6–7? (Hint: where does the "new heart" come from?)

☐ **TUESDAY** | Utter Lostness; Allegory of Unfaithfulness
Ezekiel 14–16; Psalm 119:1–64

- Human righteousness—even of great saints—is not transferable (Ezekiel 14:14), so who is left to save us (Ezekiel 16:63)?
- Chapter 16 uses two allegories: What is the first comparison in verses 1–43; the second in verses 44–58?
- What parallels do you see between Ezekiel 16:63 and Ephesians 2:8–9?

☐ **WEDNESDAY** | Personal Responsibility; Lament for Princes
Ezekiel 17–19

- How does Jesus fulfill the picture painted in Ezekiel 17:22–24? (Compare with Isaiah 53:2 and Matthew 13:31–32.)
- What bearing does Ezekiel 18:20 have on political and judicial systems?
- What fundamental truth about God do you find in Ezekiel 18:23 and 32 (see 2 Peter 3:9)? Does this match with your beliefs about him?

☐ **THURSDAY** | Rebellious Israel; Sword of Judgment; In the Gap
Ezekiel 20–22; Psalm 119:65–120

- In what ways do God's people in modern times sometimes echo Ezekiel 20:32?
- How have you seen the theme of Ezekiel 21:26 (Matthew 23:12; 1 Peter 5:6) illustrated in your experience?
- "Standing in the gap" (Ezekiel 22:30) has become a catch phrase for intercession. Who needs you to "stand in the gap" for them today (Psalm 106:23; James 5:16)?

☐ **FRIDAY** | Unfaithful Sisters; Tyre to be Destroyed
Ezekiel 23–26; Psalm 119:121–176

- What do you conclude about God's love for his people when he uses marriage and adultery to depict his affection and sense of betrayal (Ezekiel 23)?
- Ezekiel lost his wife (Ezekiel 24:18); who else lost his "wife" (24:20–24)?

- Tyre was destroyed just as predicted (Ezekiel 26:12–14); history tells us its buildings were thrown into the sea to make a causeway to the island. Are you trusting God for his Word to be fulfilled to you?

☐ **WEEKEND** | Tyre, Sidon, and Egypt Judged; Watchman; Shepherds
| **Ezekiel 27–34**

- Many see a strong parallel to the fall of the king of Tyre (Ezekiel 28:11–19) and the fall of Satan.
- How is Pharaoh's boast about the Nile (Ezekiel 29:3, 9–10) similar to ways we can erroneously take credit for God's gifts?
- How is Ezekiel like a watchman who guards a city (Ezekiel 33:1–9)? How are we like that watchman?
- What similarities do you see in Ezekiel 33:13 and 1 John 2:3–6?
- Here is a warning to everyone who serves God's people: He loves his own, and you must too (Ezekiel 34:1–6; 1 Peter 5:2–4).
- Who do you think is the one shepherd (Ezekiel 34:23–24), called "David," the future prince and shepherd of God's people (hint: John 10:11–16)?

THIS WEEK'S NOTES AND REFLECTIONS

Complete Track

MONDAY	Ezekiel 35-38
TUESDAY	Ezekiel 39-41; Psalms 120-121
WEDNESDAY	Ezekiel 42-45
THURSDAY	Ezekiel 46-48; Daniel 1
FRIDAY	Daniel 2-4; Psalms 122-124
WEEKEND	Daniel 5-12

Look for...

• Dry bones come to life—a symbol of Israel's return
• Vision of a new temple, renamed Jerusalem
• God's helping Daniel interpret the king's dreams
• Deliverance from a fiery furnace
• Handwriting on the wall
• Daniel in the lion's den
• Messiah, "Son of Man," Anointed One predicted

Activity

God used pivotal experiences in Israel's history to shape their identity: the exodus from Egypt, the conquest of Canaan, and the exile in Babylon, to name a few. Similarly, we all have defining moments in our own lives that determine the path we take. In the next few weeks, reflect on what those have been in your life. What resulting resolves have you made— what "stakes in the ground" have you driven—because of those pivotal experiences?

This Week's Prayer

Pray this prayer throughout the week: *"God, open my eyes to my defining moments and help me live the mission that flows out of them."*

□ **MONDAY** | ## Edom Warned; Valley of Dry Bones
Ezekiel 35–38

- What is Edom's sinful attitude in Ezekiel 35:15, which we too should avoid (hint: Proverbs 24:17–18)?
- What parallels do you see in Ezekiel 36:25–28 and 2 Corinthians 5:17?
- The "dry bones" vision (Ezekiel 37:1–14) is one of Ezekiel's most memorable, stressing a repeated theme: God's people will return.

□ **TUESDAY** | ## Gog Destroyed; New Temple
Ezekiel 39–41; Psalms 120–121

- The horrors described in Ezekiel 39 emphasize the price paid for sin. How does Jesus say something not that different in Matthew 5:29–30?
- How is Ezekiel 39:29 similar to Joel 2:28–32 (and Acts 2:1–4, 16–21)?
- The details for this future temple (Ezekiel 40–42) could be literal (though curiously no height measurements are given) or symbolic of God's perfect coming kingdom.

□ **WEDNESDAY** | ## Glory of the Lord; The Prince and the Priests
Ezekiel 42–45

- The "glory of the LORD" (Ezekiel 43:1–5), which earlier left the temple, returns; how was this "glory" manifest in Jesus (John 1:14; 2 Peter 1:16–18)?
- Why is this prince (Ezekiel 44:3) *not* Messiah, based on Ezekiel 45:22 and 46:16?
- What is a modern application of the principle in Ezekiel 45:9–10?

□ **THURSDAY** | ## Offerings; River from the Temple; Daniel's Character
Ezekiel 46–48; Daniel 1

- What parallels can you make to the water (Ezekiel 47:1–12) flowing from the temple and the "living water" mentioned elsewhere in Scripture (Isaiah 12:2–3; John 7:38; Revelation 22:1–5)?
- How does Jerusalem's new name (Ezekiel 48:35) fit with Revelation 21:1–4?
- Though educated in a pagan, secular environment, Daniel's character (Daniel 1:8) and close connection to God (1:17) enabled him to have the best of both worlds (1:19–20). How has God used even secular culture to further his purposes in your life? How is secular culture a danger?

☐ **FRIDAY** | **Dream Revealed; Fiery Furnace; the King Humbled**
Daniel 2–4; Psalms 122–124

- In addition to being a man of faith, what else did Daniel possess (Daniel 2:14)?
- Where are many of God's "revealed mysteries" (Daniel 2:28) today (Deuteronomy 29:29; Ephesians 3:2–6)?
- What important principle about faith is contained in Daniel 3:17–18 (especially the first few words of verse 18)?

☐ **WEEKEND** | **Fiery Furnace; Sin Confessed; Anointed One to Come**
Daniel 5–12

- Will God *always* do what he did in Daniel 6:22? (Hint: compare with Hebrews 11:36–39.)
- How does Jesus apply Daniel 7:13–14 in Mark 14:62?
- What general principles about confessing our sins can you get from Daniel 9:4–19?
- Most scholars identify Daniel 9:25–26 with Jesus; what event in Jesus' life do you suppose the "cutting off" refers to?
- How does Daniel 10:5, 12–13 illustrate the spiritual realities described in Ephesians 6:12?

THIS WEEK'S NOTES AND REFLECTIONS

Complete Track

HOSEA; JOEL; AMOS; PSALMS 125-132

MONDAY	Hosea 1-4; Psalms 125-126
TUESDAY	Hosea 5-8; Psalms 127-128
WEDNESDAY	Hosea 9-12; Psalms 129-130
THURSDAY	Hosea 13-14; Joel 1-3
FRIDAY	Amos 1-3; Psalms 131-132
WEEKEND	Amos 4-9

Look for...
- A marriage that illustrates God's love to unfaithful Israel
- A swarm of locusts that brings judgment
- The promise of the Holy Spirit to be poured out on all
- Contempt of the poor and injustice that angers God

Activity
God used pivotal experiences in Israel's history to shape their identity: the exodus from Egypt, the conquest of Canaan, and the exile in Babylon, to name a few. Similarly, we all have defining moments in our own lives that determine the path we take. In the next few weeks, reflect on what those have been in your life. What resulting resolves have you made— what "stakes in the ground" have you driven—because of those pivotal experiences?

This Week's Prayer
Pray this prayer throughout the week: *"God, open my eyes to my defining moments and help me live the mission that flows out of them."*

☐ **MONDAY** | Hosea's Marriage
Hosea 1–4; Psalms 125–126

- What spiritual truth did Hosea's highly unusual marriage (Hosea 1:2–3; 3:1–5) illustrate?
- The adultery in this image (Hosea 2:5) compares to what practice (2:8, 13)?
- How does the New Testament use Hosea 2:23 in Romans 9:23–25 and 1 Peter 2:9–10?
- How are the first few words of Hosea 4:6 still true today?

☐ **TUESDAY** | Rejection and Judgment
Hosea 5–8; Psalms 127–128

- How is it possible to find refuge in God (Hosea 6:1–3) when he has been the one punishing?
- What specific sins are being committed according to Hosea 7:1–7?
- What does the common saying about "reaping the whirlwind" (Hosea 8:7) mean?

☐ **WEDNESDAY** | Israel's Sin; God's Love
Hosea 9–12; Psalms 129–130

- Rejecting God leads to rejecting his messengers (Hosea 9:7–8); how is that done today (see 1 John 4:6)?
- Hosea 10:4 sounds too modern!
- How bad were the "days of Gibeah" (Hosea 10:9; also 9:9; see Judges 19:20–30)?
- What are the parallels between God's love for Israel (and rescue from Egypt) in Hosea 11:1 and Matthew 2:15?
- What are the similarities between Hosea 12:6 and Micah 6:8?

☐ **THURSDAY** | Coming Restoration; Invasion of Locusts
Hosea 13–14; Joel 1–3

- What is the theological implication of Hosea 13:4 and 2 Peter 1:1?
- Hosea 14:4–8 is still awaiting complete fulfillment; how is it partly fulfilled through the church (Romans 11:1–5)?
- The locust swarm (Joel 1:4) could be literal bugs or military invaders (1:6; 2:20).
- How does Joel 2:28–32 compare with Acts 2:17–21?

☐ **FRIDAY** | ## Day of the Lord
Amos 1–3; Psalms 131–132

- All the nations in Amos 1 surround Israel; how might this be a set up for the punch line in Amos 2:4 and 6?
- What economic and moral failures do you see in Amos 2:6–8?
- How does Amos's rhetorical question about human interaction in Amos 3:3 echo a truth about human-divine interaction as well?

☐ **WEEKEND** | ## Call to Repent; The Plumb Line; David's Tent Restored
Amos 4–9

- How does Matthew 8:10–12 illustrate Amos 5:18?
- How does the principle in 1 Corinthians 10:12 apply to Amos 6:1?
- What's the point of comparing God to a builder with a plumb line (Amos 7:7–8)? What is that plumb line today?
- People who reject God sometimes get their wish—his absence (Amos 8:11–12).
- How did the early church understand the promise of Amos 9:11–12 (see Acts 15:13–19)?

THIS WEEK'S NOTES AND REFLECTIONS

_____
_____
_____
_____
_____
_____
_____
_____
_____
_____
_____
_____
_____

OTC

Complete Track

OBADIAH; JONAH; MICAH; NAHUM; HABAKKUK;
ZEPHANIAH; HAGGAI; PSALMS 133–137

MONDAY	Obadiah; Jonah 1–4; Psalms 133–134
TUESDAY	Micah 1–4
WEDNESDAY	Micah 5–7; Psalm 135
THURSDAY	Nahum 1–3; Psalm 136
FRIDAY	Habakkuk 1–3; Psalm 137
WEEKEND	Zephaniah 1–3; Haggai 1–2

Look for. . .

• A reluctant prophet swallowed by a fish
• Swords to be turned into plowshares
• A prediction that Messiah will be born in Bethlehem
• God's using an evil nation to punish Israel
• God's certain triumph at the end of history

Activity

All of the prophets received a call from God to do their ministry. God was
very specific, giving them their message and empowering them to speak.
Today, we who follow Christ have the same Holy Spirit. He may not give
us a prophetic message, but he does lead us and guide us into acts of
service. What are some assignments God has given you these days? They
may be ministry, family, personal, or career related. Can you name them?
How are you doing at fulfilling them?

This Week's Prayer

Pray this prayer throughout the week: *"God, make my assignments from you
clear, my heart surrendered, and my obedience complete."*

☐ **MONDAY** | ## Nineveh Repents—God Relents—Jonah Vents
Obadiah; Jonah 1–4; Psalms 133–134

- Edom (Obadiah 1) was another name for Esau (Obadiah 6; Genesis 25:29–30), the twin brother of Jacob (Obadiah 10), both sons of Isaac—and perpetual enemies.
- Does Jesus agree with Obadiah 15 in Matthew 7:2?
- The central message about God's attitude toward the lost is in Jonah 4:2 (2 Peter 3:9); how does Jonah's attitude toward his enemies who have repented compare to the older brother in Luke 15:28–32?
- How did Jesus use Jonah's story in Matthew 12:38–41?

☐ **TUESDAY** | ## False Leaders/Prophets Denounced
Micah 1–4

- Micah uses several plays on words in Micah 1; check margin notes in your Bible—the city names in Hebrew sound like proclaimed judgments.
- How are the leaders in Micah 3:9–12 like those in Matthew 7:21–23?
- The peace of Micah 4:3 (inscribed at the United Nations) will only come when God rules (4:2, 5). Does that mean we shouldn't work for peace in the meantime (see Matthew 5:9)?

☐ **WEDNESDAY** | ## Messiah Born in Bethlehem; Walk Humbly with God
Micah 5–7; Psalm 135

- What amazing prophecy is found in Micah 5:2 (see Matthew 2:6)?
- Micah 6:8 is a great summary of all the Prophets. What parts of that message do you think still apply today?
- What parallels do you observe between Micah 6:13–16 and Deuteronomy 28:38–42, 45–52?
- How does Jesus use Micah 7:6 in Matthew 10:34–36?
- What traits of God in Micah 7:18–20 do you need right now?

☐ **THURSDAY** | ## Nineveh to Fall
Nahum 1–3; Psalm 136

- Nineveh, which repented when Jonah confronted it, now stands condemned (Nahum 1:1).
- God never changes; how are his traits in Nahum 1:2–8 seen today?
- God declared himself "against" Nineveh (Nahum 2:13; 3:5); what did its people do that provoked him? (Hint: see 1:14; 3:1–4.)

☐ **FRIDAY** | How Long, O Lord?
Habakkuk 1–3; Psalm 137

- How would you put Habakkuk's complaint in Habakkuk 1:2–4 into modern terms?
- How is it fair for God, who is perfectly just, to use an unjust nation to punish Israel (Habakkuk 1:6; but see 3:16)?
- Faith was the way through the crisis (Habakkuk 2:4); how does the New Testament echo this truth in Romans 1:17; Galatians 3:11; and Hebrews 10:37–38?
- How does Habakkuk 3:17–18 compare with Philippians 4:11–13?

☐ **WEEKEND** | God Judges and Encourages; The House of the Lord
Zephaniah 1–3; Haggai 1–2

- What wrong thoughts about God do people have in Zephaniah 1:12 (Genesis 18:25; 2 Peter 3:3–4)?
- Can you imagine God doing Zephaniah 3:17 with *you*?
- What spiritual principle does "building God's house first" (Haggai 1:2–11) illustrate (see Matthew 6:31–33)?
- How expansive will God's dominion be according to Haggai 2:6–7?
- Do you think God sometimes uses hardships (Haggai 2:7) to get our attention today?

THIS WEEK'S NOTES AND REFLECTIONS

OTC

Complete Track

ZECHARIAH; MALACHI; EZRA; PSALMS 138-144

MONDAY	Zechariah 1-5
TUESDAY	Zechariah 6-9; Psalms 138-139
WEDNESDAY	Zechariah 10-14
THURSDAY	Malachi 1-4; Psalms 140-141
FRIDAY	Ezra 1-4; Psalms 142-144
WEEKEND	Ezra 5-10

Look for...
• Prophecies of the "Branch" and a king coming on a donkey
• Israel to weep over "piercing" their God
• God's invitation to Israel to test his lavish generosity
• Temple rebuilt despite opposition
• Ezra's great example of public confession

Activity
All of the prophets received a call from God to do their ministry. God was very specific, giving them their message and empowering them to speak. Today, we who follow Christ have the same Holy Spirit. He may not give us a prophetic message, but he does lead us and guide us into acts of service. What are some assignments God has given you these days? They may be ministry, family, personal, or career related. Can you name them? How are you doing at fulfilling them?

This Week's Prayer
Pray this prayer throughout the week: *"God, make my assignments from you clear, my heart surrendered, and my obedience complete."*

☐ **MONDAY** | ## Measuring Line; Not by Might or Power but by My Spirit
Zechariah 1–5

- What might be the symbolic meaning of "measuring" the restored and blessed Jerusalem (Zechariah 2:1; Revelation 21:15)?
- If the "apple of the eye" is the sensitive iris, what does Zechariah 2:8 imply?
- How does Jesus fulfill Zechariah 2:11 and 3:8–9?
- How have you seen the truth of Zechariah 4:6 in your life?
- Like a billboard (Zechariah 5:2–3), God's judgment will be seen by all.

☐ **TUESDAY** | ## The Branch; King and Kingdom to Come
Zechariah 6–9; Psalms 138–139

- The king couldn't be a priest nor a priest be a king; the "Branch" (Zechariah 6:12–13) is both—so who is he (see John 18:37 and Hebrews 4:14)?
- How is Zechariah 7:13 like Matthew 10:32–33?
- Do you think Zechariah 7:9–10 and 8:16–17 apply today?
- Jew and Gentile alike will be part of God's "new community" according to Zechariah 8:20–23.
- Rather than riding arrogantly on a war horse, how does Israel's King of kings arrive (Zechariah 9:9)?

☐ **WEDNESDAY** | ## 30 Silver Pieces; Piercing and Weeping
Zechariah 10–14

- What similar thing did Jesus and Zechariah see (Zechariah 10:2; Matthew 9:36)?
- What parallels exist between how people valued Zechariah and how they valued Jesus (Zechariah 11:12–13; Matthew 26:15; and 27:9–10)?
- When did Israel "pierce" their God (Zechariah 12:10; John 19:37; Revelation 1:7) or strike their shepherd (Zechariah 13:7; Matthew 26:31)?

☐ **THURSDAY** | ## Empty, Complacent Religion Condemned
Malachi 1–4; Psalms 140–141

- What is a contemporary example of Malachi 1:8 and 14?
- What are some principles from Malachi 2:6–7 a small group leader can use?
- What is similar in Malachi 2:13–16 and 1 Peter 3:7?
- What is a timeless principle about God's generosity in Malachi 3:10–11?
- How is Malachi 3:16 similar to Hebrews 10:25?

☐ **FRIDAY** | Some Exiles Return; Temple Construction Begins
Ezra 1–4; Psalms 142–144

- Although he was a pagan, what political gain might have motivated Cyrus's decree in Ezra 1:1–2?
- Mixed emotions probably came from comparing this inferior temple to its predecessor (Ezra 3:12).
- What spiritual, as well as political, realities might lie behind Ezra 4:1–5?

☐ **WEEKEND** | Temple Finished; Ezra Arrives; Foreign Wives Sent Away
Ezra 5–10

- Agents of kings in those days were called "the king's eyes"; what then is the significance of Ezra 5:3–5?
- Darius (Ezra 6:1) and Artaxerxes (7:1) believed in many gods; why do you think they decreed as they did (Ezra 6:10; 7:23)?
- What are some principles of public confession evident in Ezra's prayer in Ezra 9:6–15? When is the last time you had a "spiritual house-cleaning" confession with God about your sin?
- The harsh but necessary action in Ezra 10:3 may have been tempered in the case of wives who had converted to Israel's God; the three-month process ensured fairness (Ezra 10:16–17).

THIS WEEK'S NOTES AND REFLECTIONS

_____
_____
_____
_____
_____
_____
_____
_____
_____
_____
_____
_____

OTC

Complete Track

NEHEMIAH; ESTHER; PSALMS 145-150

MONDAY	Nehemiah 1-3
TUESDAY	Nehemiah 4-6; Psalm 145
WEDNESDAY	Nehemiah 7-8
THURSDAY	Nehemiah 9-11; Psalms 146-147
FRIDAY	Nehemiah 12-13; Psalms 148-150
WEEKEND	Esther 1-10

Look for...
- Nehemiah's getting permission from a pagan king to rebuild the walls
- Rebuilding Israel's character as important as building stone walls
- People pledging obedience, yet still needing grace
- A beauty pageant leading to Esther's rise to prominence
- God's working behind the scenes to bring about deliverance for his people

Activity
With this week's reading, you've completed the Old Testament Challenge. *Congratulations!* From the beginning of creation to Israel's return from captivity, you've seen God at work building his "new community." Just as ancient Israel was on a journey with God, you've been on a journey. What have been highlights from your reading? What principles or verses from God's Word do you want to keep in focus as a reminder of what you've learned?

This Week's Prayer
Pray this prayer: *"God, long ago against impossible odds you built a kingdom; keep building it now through me."*

☐ MONDAY | Nehemiah Returns, Wall Construction Begins
Nehemiah 1–3

- What principles of confession do you see in Nehemiah 1:5–11?
- How long do you suppose it took to see an answer to the prayer in Nehemiah 2:4–5?
- What effect on workmanship do you think it had to assign the section of wall near a worker's home for him (or *her*, Nehemiah 3:12!) to rebuild (Nehemiah 3:10, 23, 28, 30)?
- What area of your life, like the wall in Jerusalem, has fallen into disrepair and needs to be rebuilt and strengthened?

☐ TUESDAY | Wall Completed; The Poor Protected
Nehemiah 4–6; Psalm 145

- Nehemiah did not retaliate, nor did he view the threat from Sanballat as against him alone. How does that backdrop affect your view of his prayer in Nehemiah 4:4–5?
- What spiritual principle can you see in the combination of human effort and trust in God in Nehemiah 4:19–20 and 6:16?
- What example of leadership do you see in Nehemiah 5:14–18?

☐ WEDNESDAY | The Law Read
Nehemiah 7–8

- How does Nehemiah 8:8 sum up what every good teacher of God's Word should do?
- When convicted of sin, what principle of Nehemiah 8:9–12 applies (see also 9:17)?
- What does obedience produce in Nehemiah 8:17? Do people see that in *you*?

☐ THURSDAY | Confession, Pledge of Obedience
Nehemiah 9–11; Psalms 146–147

- How might acknowledgment of sin (Nehemiah 9:5–37) help solidify a vow of obedience (9:38 and 10:28–39)?
- What parallels can you make between Israel's history as recounted in Nehemiah 9 and your own history with God?
- People had to resettle in Jerusalem to make it strong (Nehemiah 11:1–2). What parallels can you make to church planting or starting a new ministry in our day?

☐ **FRIDAY** | Dedication and Reforms; Queen Vashti Deposed
Nehemiah 12–13; Psalms 148–150

- Nehemiah 12:27–47 encourages instrumental and vocal music in worship of God; are you "singing and making melody in your heart" (Ephesians 5:19)?
- Sabbath desecration (Nehemiah 13:15–22) violated Israel's solemn oath made earlier (10:31); how do Jesus (Matthew 12:1–12) and Paul (Colossians 2:16–17) modify current Sabbath practice?

☐ **WEEKEND** | Esther is Queen; Haman Schemes; Jews Triumph
Esther 1–10

- How does Xerxes' intimidation (Esther 1:17–22) differ from God's design for husbands (Ephesians 5:25; Colossians 3:19)?
- What position do you hold (Esther 4:14) that God may want to use to accomplish purposes beyond you?
- Have you ever had to trust God for your life and cast yourself solely on his mercy (Esther 4:16)?
- Who are the converts in Esther 8:17 *ultimately* impressed with?
- The final victory (Esther 10:3) is clear evidence of God's actions.
- Do you notice something strange about the book of Esther? The word "God" never occurs! Yet his activity is on every page—just as it is in your life!

THIS WEEK'S NOTES AND REFLECTIONS

_____
_____
_____
_____
_____
_____
_____
_____
_____
_____
_____
_____

OTC

PART 2

READING GUIDE | **Fast Track**

32 WEEK SUMMARY

☐ **WEEK 1**   Genesis 1–2; Job 38–39

☐ **WEEK 2**   Genesis 3–4; 6; 8–9

☐ **WEEK 3**   Genesis 12–17; 21–23; 25:1–11

☐ **WEEK 4**   Genesis 24–25; 28–29; 32–33; 37; 39; 41

☐ **WEEK 5**   Exodus 1–7:13; 8:1–15; 12–14

☐ **WEEK 6**   Exodus 18–20; 23–24; Deuteronomy 5

☐ **WEEK 7**   Exodus 15–17; 32; Numbers 11–14; 20:1–13

☐ **WEEK 8**   Exodus 25; 35–36; 40; Leviticus 16; 26

☐ **WEEK 9**   Deuteronomy 1; 4; 6; 13; 15; 18; 24; 29–30

☐ **WEEK 10**   Joshua 1–6; 10; 14; 23

☐ **WEEK 11**   Deuteronomy 7–9; Numbers 25; Leviticus 18; Joshua 7; 9; Isaiah 2

☐ **WEEK 12**   Judges 2–8

☐ **WEEK 13**   Judges 11–16; Ruth

☐ **WEEK 14**   1 Samuel 1–4; 7–8

☐ **WEEK 15**   1 Samuel 9–10; 13; 15–16; 18; 24; 28; 31

☐ **WEEK 16**   Isaiah 9; 11; 53; Zechariah 12:10; Micah 5:1–2; Ezekiel 37; Daniel 7:1–14

☐ **WEEK 17**   1 Samuel 17; 2 Samuel 5–6; 9; 11–15; 18; Psalms 18; 23; 51

☐ **WEEK 18**   Psalms 33–35; 42; 58; 100; 103; 117; 137

☐ **WEEK 19**   Psalms 30; 69; 74; 83; 94; 96; 119:1–112

☐ **WEEK 20**   Song of Songs

☐ **WEEK 21**   1 Kings 1–3; Proverbs 1; 5–7; 10–11; 24–26

☐ **WEEK 22**   Numbers 33:50–56; Deuteronomy 16:21–17:20; 1 Kings 4:20–34; 8–11

☐ **WEEK 23**   Job 1–4; 6; 8; 11; 19; 23; 38:1–7; 40; 42

☐ **WEEK 24**   1 Kings 12; 14–16; 2 Chronicles 14–16

☐ **WEEK 25**   1 Kings 17–19:14

☐ **WEEK 26**   1 Kings 19:15–21; 2 Kings 2–6

☐ **WEEK 27**   The Book of Amos

☐ **WEEK 28**   Isaiah 2–6; 40; 43; 56; 66

☐ **WEEK 29**   2 Chronicles 30–32; Isaiah 7–8; 36–39

☐ **WEEK 30**   Isaiah 1; Micah

☐ **WEEK 31**   Jeremiah 1–2; 18–20; 23; 31:31–34; 37–38; Lamentations 3:22–33

☐ **WEEK 32**   2 Kings 25; Jeremiah 29:1–23; Daniel 9:1–19; Ezra 1:1–8; Nehemiah 1–2; Malachi 4; Psalms 78–79; Hebrews 11

Fast Track

GOD'S GREATEST DREAM: GENESIS 1-2; JOB 38-39

> **FIRST READING** Genesis 1; Psalm 1
>
> **SECOND READING** Genesis 2; Psalm 8
>
> **THIRD READING** Job 38-39; Psalm 19

Look for...

- God creates the universe
- God makes man and woman "in his image"
- God's creation is "good"—becomes "very good," once people arrive
- God and the man and woman enjoy a perfect relationship

Activity

This week, you're on a "God-hunt." Imagine you know very little about God. What do these early chapters of the Bible teach you about him? What are his likes and dislikes? How powerful is he? What is his nature? Also, pay attention to what you see of God in your everyday life through such things as answered prayer, experiences of beauty, or a prompting to reach out to someone.

This Week's Prayer

Pray this prayer throughout the week: *"Heavenly Father, I want to know you through your Word and meet you in my life. What do you want to teach me about yourself today?"*

☐ **FIRST READING** | Genesis 1; Psalm 1

- What hint about the "community nature" of God (the Trinity) can you see in Genesis 1:2 and 26–27?
- If God is invisible, what do you think "created in the image of God" means?
- Why do you think creation is called "very good" only *after* humans are on the scene?
- How would we all treat each other differently if we really believed we were made in God's image—even with all our faults?

☐ **SECOND READING** | Genesis 2; Psalm 8

- Are God's limitations on eating from the tree of knowledge of good and evil (Genesis 2:17) proof he is stingy and has a "restrictive" bent (hint: see verse 16)?
- What clue about our need for community is contained in Genesis 2:18? Is a spouse the only solution for this need (hint: see 1 John 4:7–8, 12)?
- What is the spiritual significance of "being naked without shame" (Genesis 2:25)?

☐ **THIRD READING** | Job 38–39; Psalm 19

- What parallels can you make between the creation account in Job and what happened in Genesis 1–2? What are some differences?
- How would you sum up what these passages teach about God's power and creativity? What about his desires for humans?

THIS WEEK'S NOTES AND REFLECTIONS

_____
_____
_____
_____
_____
_____
_____
_____
_____
_____

Fast Track

COMMUNITY BUSTERS: GENESIS 3-4; 6; 8-9

> **FIRST READING** Genesis 3; Psalm 32
>
> **SECOND READING** Genesis 4; Psalm 10
>
> **THIRD READING** Genesis 6; 8-9; Psalm 14

Look for. . .

- Satan distorts what God says
- Humans disobey and fall from innocence
- God provides a "covering" for sin, at the expense of innocent life
- Sin spreads and corrupts the earth
- The great Flood

Activity

This week, you're on a "God-hunt." Imagine you know very little about God. What do these early chapters of the Bible teach you about him? What are his likes and dislikes? How powerful is he? What is his nature? Also, pay attention to what you see of God in your everyday life through such things as answered prayer, experiences of beauty, or a prompting to reach out to someone.

This Week's Prayer

Pray this prayer throughout the week: *"Heavenly Father, I want to know you through your Word and meet you in my life. What do you want to teach me about yourself today?"*

☐ **FIRST READING** | Genesis 3; Psalm 32

- How did the serpent twist God's words in Genesis 3:1 and 4 (compare Genesis 2:16–17)?
- In spite of the curses, how did God show grace after the Fall? What does this tell you about him?
- What New Testament event does Genesis 3:15 foreshadow?

☐ **SECOND READING** | Genesis 4; Psalm 10

- In Genesis 4, sin spreads from the individual to the family. How are families you know still experiencing the fallout from sin today?
- In addition to the offering itself, what (or rather, who) was "out of favor" (Genesis 4:4–5)?
- What details from the story of Cain and Abel does Hebrews 11:4 stress?
- What example of sin's deteriorating effects do you see in Genesis 4:19, 23–24?

☐ **THIRD READING** | Genesis 6, 8–9; Psalm 14

- What about Noah made him the exception to the rest of the world?
- Why do you suppose God waited so long (120 years) to begin the Flood after telling Noah it was coming?
- What does it tell you about God's character that so many years went by before he judged sin? How are you doing these days in mimicking God's patience even when retribution is justified?

THIS WEEK'S NOTES AND REFLECTIONS

_____
_____
_____
_____
_____
_____
_____
_____
_____

OTC

Fast Track

IT'S TIME TO DTR (DEFINE THE RELATIONSHIP): GENESIS 12–17; 21–23; 25:1–11

FIRST READING	Genesis 12–14; Psalm 17
SECOND READING	Genesis 15–17; 18:1–15; Psalm 47
THIRD READING	Genesis 21–23; 25:1–11; Psalm 105

Look for...

- The call of Abraham (Abram) to begin a "new community"
- God promises an heir but takes a long time
- Sarah and Abraham laugh
- Promised son Isaac is finally born
- Isaac is "sacrificed" and returned

Activity

This week, you're on a "God-hunt." Imagine you know very little about God. What do these early chapters of the Bible teach you about him? What are his likes and dislikes? How powerful is he? What is his nature? Also, pay attention to what you see of God in your everyday life through such things as answered prayer, experiences of beauty, or a prompting to reach out to someone.

This Week's Prayer

Pray this prayer throughout the week: *"Heavenly Father, I want to know you through your Word and meet you in my life. What do you want to teach me about yourself today?"*

☐ **FIRST READING** | Genesis 12–14; Psalm 17

- Though Abram was "chosen" out of the nations, who else did God want to bless through his offspring (Genesis 12:2–3)? Compare this "Old Testament Great Commission" to the New Testament version in Matthew 28:18–20.
- What comparison does the New Testament make to Melchizedek in Hebrews 7:1–22?
- What biblical precedent of handling an increase of wealth do you see in Abraham's actions in Genesis 14:20?

☐ **SECOND READING** | Genesis 15–17; 18:1–15; Psalm 47

- What "saved" Abraham (Abram) according to Genesis 15:6?
- How do Romans 4 and Galatians 3:6–14 shed more light on the significance of God's dealings with Abraham?
- How does experiencing God's favor inspire us to reach others with that love? Why do we sometimes lose concern for the lost?

☐ **THIRD READING** | Genesis 21–23; 25:1–11; Psalm 105

- Based on what you've seen of Abraham and Sarah's maturity and faithfulness, what is the significance of the word "gracious" in Genesis 21:1? What do you learn about God from this passage?
- What wordplay is made on Isaac's name (which means "laughter") in Genesis 21:6 (going back to 18:10–15)?
- Genesis 22 contains a powerful "type" (metaphor) for the future sacrifice and resurrection of God's other "miracle" son, Jesus.
- What parallels in language and imagery do you see between the sacrifice of Isaac and the sacrifice of Jesus in John 3:16; Romans 8:32; and Hebrews 11:17–19?

THIS WEEK'S NOTES AND REFLECTIONS

_____

_____

_____

_____

_____

_____

_____

Fast Track

GOD IS WITH US: GENESIS 24-25; 28-29; 32-33; 37; 39; 41

FIRST READING	Genesis 24–25; 28; Psalm 16
SECOND READING	Genesis 29; 32–33; Psalm 22
THIRD READING	Genesis 37; 39; 41; Psalm 73

Look for. . .

- Twins Jacob and Esau's stormy relationship
- Jacob the "Deceiver" pursued by God
- Jacob's name changed to Israel after heavenly dream
- Jacob's son Joseph (of *Amazing Technicolor Dreamcoat* fame) dreams of greatness
- Joseph stands strong against Potiphar's wife and rises to power in Egypt

Activity

This week, you're on a "God-hunt." Imagine you know very little about God. What do these early chapters of the Bible teach you about him? What are his likes and dislikes? How powerful is he? What is his nature? Also, pay attention to what you see of God in your everyday life through such things as answered prayer, experiences of beauty, or a prompting to reach out to someone.

This Week's Prayer

Pray this prayer throughout the week: *"Heavenly Father, I want to know you through your Word and meet you in my life. What do you want to teach me about yourself today?"*

☐ **FIRST READING** | **Genesis 24–25; 28; Psalm 16**

- Malachi 1:2–5 harks back to God's kindness to Jacob over Esau as a warning not to be smug. How can we be secure and yet avoid becoming spiritually complacent in God's love?

- Paul notes in Romans 9:6–16 how the scheming Jacob was blessed in spite of his character defects. What lesson about God—and grace—do you take to heart from that fact?

- How did Jesus use the story of Jacob's dream (Genesis 28:10–19) to describe his own role as a "bridge" between God and humans (John 1:50–51)?

☐ **SECOND READING** | **Genesis 29; 32–33; Psalm 22**

- What have you seen in Jacob's life that explains his mindset in Genesis 32:7?

- By contrast, what faith lessons do you learn as you read his prayer in Genesis 32:9–12?

- The "man" Jacob wrestles with is clearly a supernatural being, who reminds him that his ultimate struggle is not with Laban or Esau but with God.

- If you were to "wrestle with God," what would be the issue?

☐ **THIRD READING** | **Genesis 37; 39; 41; Psalm 73**

- Joseph receives two "demotions," yet how does God work even in those injustices (Genesis 37:2–7, 20–23)? What does this teach you about God's power—both the extent and its limitations—in the face of evil?

- What strong warnings concerning those who interpret dreams are given in Deuteronomy 13:1–5 and 18:9–13?

- What other leadership qualities did Joseph exhibit (Genesis 41:33–40)?

- How does Acts 7:9–10 summarize the events of Joseph's life up to this point?

THIS WEEK'S NOTES AND REFLECTIONS

_____

_____

_____

_____

_____

_____

OTC

Fast Track

GOD THE DELIVERER: EXODUS 1-7:13; 8:1-15; 12-14

FIRST READING	Exodus 1-3; Psalm 90
SECOND READING	Exodus 4-7:13; Psalm 37
THIRD READING	Exodus 8:1-15; 12-14; Psalm 136

Look for...

- Hebrews (Israelites) become slaves
- Midwives defy Pharaoh's edict
- Moses, a Jew, is raised as a son of Pharaoh
- Moses and the burning bush
- The first Passover
- Miraculous crossing of the Red Sea on dry land

Activity

Continue your "God-hunt" from previous weeks. What are these early chapters of the Bible teaching you about God's nature? Where do you see God in your everyday life through such things as answered prayer, experiences of beauty, or a prompting to reach out to someone?

This Week's Prayer

Pray this prayer throughout the week: *"Heavenly Father, I want to know you through your Word and meet you in my life. What do you want to teach me about yourself today?"*

☐ **FIRST READING** | Exodus 1–3; Psalm 90

- What subtle point might the writer be making by including the names of the Hebrew midwives in the first chapter but not Pharaoh's?
- What do you think it means to "fear" God as in Exodus 1:17, 21?
- God can only define himself in terms of himself ("I AM WHO I AM," Exodus 3:14); what is the implication when Jesus defines himself as he does in John 8:56–59?

☐ **SECOND READING** | Exodus 4–7:13; Psalm 37

- What similarities exist between how God used miracles in Exodus 4:1–9 (to authenticate Moses' message) and how Jesus used miracles in John 2:18–23; 10:25–26, 37–38?
- What parallel can you make to your own life concerning God's words in Exodus 4:10–12?
- In Exodus 6:1–8, the statement "I am the LORD" is repeated four times; what does God reveal to Moses about himself in response to Moses' complaints?
- What would hearing God say "I am the LORD" mean to you as you face your current challenges?

☐ **THIRD READING** | Exodus 8:1–15; 12–14; Psalm 136

- How did God show his faithfulness to the Israelites in Exodus 8:23 and 9:4, 26? Does God always do this (Matthew 5:45)?
- What does the Passover represent and why was it to be remembered (Exodus 12:26–27)?
- How did God provide for the Israelites as they left Egypt (Exodus 12:35–36)? How might their years of slavery justify that provision?
- How do you think your life would change if you saw God do a miracle like the parting of the Red Sea (Exodus 14:31)? Would you ever doubt God again? (After you answer, read Exodus 16:3!)

THIS WEEK'S NOTES AND REFLECTIONS

Fast Track

GOD THE LAWGIVER: EXODUS 18-20; 23-24; DEUTERONOMY 5

> **FIRST READING** Exodus 18-19; Psalm 29
>
> **SECOND READING** Exodus 20; Deuteronomy 5; Psalm 68
>
> **THIRD READING** Exodus 23-24; Psalm 46

Look for. . .

- Moses learns to delegate
- God thunders on Mount Sinai
- The Ten Commandments

Activity

Observe the various laws you obey—or disobey—in the course of an average day (speed limits, paying sales tax, not stealing, voting, etc.). What principles or values can you identify that lie behind the laws? What do you learn about yourself as you react to these laws?

This Week's Prayer

Pray this prayer throughout the week: *"Heavenly Father, use your laws to teach me about holiness, reveal my sin, and help me follow you with my whole heart."*

☐ **FIRST READING** | **Exodus 18–19; Psalm 29**

- Is there a situation in your life, work, or ministry where Jethro's advice to Moses in Exodus 18:17–23 could be applicable?
- How would the terrifying experiences described in Exodus 19 help the people understand God's holiness? Why would that be important to their spiritual development?
- How have you been too casual about God's holiness lately?

☐ **SECOND READING** | **Exodus 20; Deuteronomy 5; Psalm 68**

- As you read through the Ten Commandments, which one causes an "ouch" factor for you? What do you believe God wants you to do in response?
- The people were afraid of God's power, but Moses said they shouldn't be (see Exodus 20:18–20); how should God's power affect us today? What about times when we don't see it?

☐ **THIRD READING** | **Exodus 23–24; Psalm 46**

- What do laws like Exodus 23:1–9 teach about the nature of God?
- Compare Exodus 24:17 with Deuteronomy 4:24 and Hebrews 12:28–29. Why do you think God revealed himself like this, as well as like the image in Exodus 24:9–11?

THIS WEEK'S NOTES AND REFLECTIONS

_____

_____

_____

_____

_____

_____

_____

_____

_____

_____

_____

_____

Fast Track

LESSONS FROM THE WILDERNESS: EXODUS 15-17; 32; NUMBERS 11-14; 20:1-13

> FIRST READING Exodus 15-17; Psalm 81
>
> SECOND READING Exodus 32; Numbers 11-12; Psalm 95
>
> THIRD READING Numbers 13-14; 20:1-13; Psalm 106

Look for...
• Manna, quail, and water are miraculously supplied in the desert
• Golden calf idolatry
• Miriam and Aaron undermine Moses' authority
• Spies explore Canaan, but the people fail to enter
• Moses disobeys God in anger and forfeits living in Canaan

Activity
Observe the various laws you obey—or disobey—in the course of an average day (speed limits, paying sales tax, not stealing, voting, etc.). What principles or values can you identify that lie behind the laws? What do you learn about yourself as you react to these laws?

This Week's Prayer
Pray this prayer throughout the week: *"Heavenly Father, use your laws to teach me about holiness, reveal my sin, and help me follow you with my whole heart."*

....

□ **FIRST READING** ▏ Exodus 15–17; Psalm 81

- After some initial excitement about God's power (Exodus 15:3–11), the Israelites soon grumble about their adversity in the desert; do you think you'd behave the same way in such circumstances?
- Exodus 15:26 states God will heal all the Israelites' diseases. Is this always true for God's people (see Job 2:7–10; 2 Corinthians 12:7–10; Philippians 2:25–30; 1 Timothy 5:23)?
- In Exodus 17:1–2 the people's request for water seems reasonable; what light does verse 7 shed on the sinful attitude behind the request?

....

□ **SECOND READING** ▏ Exodus 32; Numbers 11–12; Psalm 95

- What is a contemporary situation similar to what prompted the people to want another god (Exodus 32:1; see also 2 Peter 3:3–4 and Matthew 24:4–13)?
- What lessons about the importance—and limits—of prayer might be learned from Moses' intercession in Exodus 32:11–14, 30–35?
- How are events in Numbers 11:25–29 like Acts 2:14–18 and 19:6?
- What racist bias (Numbers 12:1) was underneath Miriam and Aaron's "spiritual sounding" complaint (verse 2)?

....

□ **THIRD READING** ▏ Numbers 13–14; 20:1–1; Psalm 106

- What important lesson does Numbers 13:33 contain about how the spies' view of themselves affected their courage?
- Do you see yourself as a "grasshopper" in an area where God sees you differently? How can you see yourself with his eyes?
- In Numbers 20:8, God gave Moses specific instructions; in verses 10–11 he disobeyed. What attitude do you sense in Moses' words, indicating the reason for God's response (verse 12)?

....

THIS WEEK'S NOTES AND REFLECTIONS

Fast Track

WHAT INDIANA JONES WAS LOOKING FOR: EXODUS 25; 35–36; 40; LEVITICUS 16; 26

FIRST READING	Exodus 25; 35; Psalm 27
SECOND READING	Exodus 36; 40; Psalm 50
THIRD READING	Leviticus 16; 26; Psalm 66

Look for...
• Tabernacle specifications
• Craftsmen equipped by the Holy Spirit to do their work
• Day of Atonement
• Blessings of obedience

Activity
Observe the various laws you obey—or disobey—in the course of an average day (speed limits, paying sales tax, not stealing, voting, etc.). What principles or values can you identify that lie behind the laws? What do you learn about yourself as you react to these laws?

This Week's Prayer
Pray this prayer throughout the week: *"Heavenly Father, use your laws to teach me about holiness, reveal my sin, and help me follow you with my whole heart."*

☐ **FIRST READING** | Exodus 25; 35; Psalm 27

- Read Exodus 35:20–29. How do you think the experience of community and worship was affected by the widespread participation of individuals?
- Besides being craftsmen, what else did God's Spirit do for Bezalel and Oholiab (Exodus 35:34)?

☐ **SECOND READING** | Exodus 36; 40; Psalm 50

- All the elements of the tabernacle had two important features: portability and stunning beauty. What might God be teaching the Israelites about his nature through these symbols?
- What lesson did the Israelites learn from Exodus 40:36–38? Why do you suppose God stopped leading them with those sensational means after they entered Canaan? Why do you think he typically doesn't use such dramatic means in our day either?

☐ **THIRD READING** | Leviticus 16; 26; Psalm 66

- God set forth one day each year for the high priest to represent the whole nation of Israel in a ceremony of atonement (called Yom Kippur). What does Hebrews 9 say about this event?
- A feast is an appointed time to remember a particular event or spiritual lesson; one of the elements of the feasts is a Sabbath, or day of rest, dedicated to the Lord. How can you incorporate "remembering" and taking Sabbaths into your rhythm of life?
- What are some examples of God's grace shown in Leviticus 26?
- What provision is made in Leviticus 26:40–45 for a person who sins?

THIS WEEK'S NOTES AND REFLECTIONS

_____

_____

_____

_____

_____

_____

_____

_____

OTC

Fast Track

CHOOSE LIFE: DEUTERONOMY 1; 4; 6; 13; 15; 18; 24; 29-30

FIRST READING	Deuteronomy 1; 4; 6; Psalm 38
SECOND READING	Deuteronomy 13; 15; 18; Psalm 39
THIRD READING	Deuteronomy 24; 29-30; Psalm 40

Look for...

- Retelling Israel's history
- Obedience commanded
- "Hear, O Israel. . ."
- Idolatry condemned
- Laws encouraging compassion
- Offer of life and blessings

Activity

Observe the various laws you obey—or disobey—in the course of an average day (speed limits, paying sales tax, not stealing, voting, etc.). What principles or values can you identify that lie behind the laws? What do you learn about yourself as you react to these laws?

This Week's Prayer

Pray this prayer throughout the week: *"Heavenly Father, use your laws to teach me about holiness, reveal my sin, and help me follow you with my whole heart."*

☐ **FIRST READING** | Deuteronomy 1; 4; 6; Psalm 38

- Why do the spiritual-sounding human additions to God's law (which produce legalism) in Deuteronomy 4:2 displease God as much as setting aside commands? (Also see Matthew 15:3–9; 23:4; Revelation 22:18–19, and Eve's additions in Genesis 3:3.)
- What does Jesus say about Deuteronomy 6:4–6 in Matthew 22:37–40?
- Where are spiritual values best modeled according to Deuteronomy 6:7? What happens when they're not modeled there?

☐ **SECOND READING** | Deuteronomy 13; 15; 18; Psalm 39

- If a fortune-teller accurately predicts the future but doesn't honor the Bible, how should we respond, based on principles from Deuteronomy 13:1–4?
- What similarities do you see between Deuteronomy 13:6–8 and Luke 12:51–53 and 14:25–26?
- What truth helps the Israelites—and us—act generously in Deuteronomy 15:4–6, 10, 14, and 18?
- Jesus quotes Deuteronomy 15:11 in John 12:8; why will there "always" be poor Israelites if God blesses obedience (see 2 Corinthians 8:13–15 and Philippians 4:12)?

☐ **THIRD READING** | Deuteronomy 24; 29–30; Psalm 40

- What compassion is engendered by Deuteronomy 24:12–15 and 19–21?
- What bearing does Deuteronomy 29:29 have on unanswered questions in your life? (Also see John 21:25; Acts 1:7; 1 Corinthians 13:12; 2 Corinthians 4:18.)
- How would you translate Deuteronomy 30:19–20 into terms that apply today?

THIS WEEK'S NOTES AND REFLECTIONS

_____

_____

_____

_____

_____

_____

_____

_____

Fast Track

THE LAW OF THE FIRST STEP: JOSHUA 1-6; 10; 14; 23

> **FIRST READING** Joshua 1-3; Psalm 114
>
> **SECOND READING** Joshua 4-6; Psalm 52
>
> **THIRD READING** Joshua 10; 14; 23; Psalm 135

Look for...

- Joshua assumes leadership: "be strong and courageous"
- In faith, Rahab the prostitute hides the spies
- Jordan River is miraculously crossed
- Jericho's walls fall down
- The sun stands still
- Joshua's farewell: "As for me and my house...."

Activity

Observe the way living things around you grow and mature: children, pets, plants, and so on. What parallels can you make between their growth—with fits and starts, beauty and bewilderment—and spiritual progress? What most frustrates you about the growth process? What is rewarding?

This Week's Prayer

Pray this prayer throughout the week: *"Heavenly Father, use the history of your people 'growing up' as a nation to teach me how to grow up as your child."*

☐ FIRST READING | Joshua 1–3; Psalm 114

- The name Joshua (Hebrew *yeh-SHU-ah*; Greek *YAY-sous* or Jesus) means, "Jehovah is salvation."
- What repeated phrases in Joshua 1:1–9 still apply to you today?
- What marks of "conversion" do you see in Rahab's life in Joshua 2:8–13; Hebrews 11:31; and James 2:25?
- Which came first in Joshua 3:13, the Jordan drying up or the priests stepping into it? What parallels can you make to a life of faith today?

☐ SECOND READING | Joshua 4–6; Psalm 52

- What lesson did God teach "all the peoples" by drying up the Jordan (Joshua 4:20–24)?
- In Joshua 5:13–15, why would God say he is not an ally (see verse 14)?
- What parallels can you make between God's leading the conquest of Canaan and God's flooding the earth in the time of Noah?
- How does Joshua 6:26 compare with 1 Kings 16:34?

☐ THIRD READING | Joshua 10; 14; 23; Psalm 135

- The miracle in Joshua 10:12–14 helped the Israelites win the battle; yet all the battles in the next chapter were fought without such obvious divine intervention. What parallel to our lives with God today can you make from these incidents?
- In Joshua 14, after forty-five years, Caleb finally receives his promised inheritance (see Numbers 14:6–9, 24; 32:11–12; Deuteronomy 1:35–36). What do you think it would be like to wait four and a half decades while being "wholeheartedly" faithful?
- What difficult assignment does Caleb ask for in Joshua 14:10–12? What does that tell you about his character?
- What would your life look like today if you made the pledge in Joshua 24:15 your own?

THIS WEEK'S NOTES AND REFLECTIONS

_____

_____

_____

_____

_____

_____

OTC

Fast Track

THE OLD TESTAMENT AND HOLY WAR: DEUTERONOMY 7–9; NUMBERS 25; LEVITICUS 18;
JOSHUA 7; 9; ISAIAH 2

FIRST READING	Deuteronomy 7–9; Psalm 9
SECOND READING	Numbers 25; Leviticus 18; Psalm 36
THIRD READING	Joshua 7; 9; Isaiah 2; Psalm 62

Look for. . .

• Canaan culture utterly wicked
• Severe temptations will overtake Israel if Canaanites remain
• God punishes Israel's disobedience as well as that of the pagans
• A new day of peace and justice promised

Activity

Observe the way living things around you grow and mature: children,
pets, plants, and so on. What parallels can you make between their
growth—with fits and starts, beauty and bewilderment—and spiritual
progress? What most frustrates you about the growth process? What is
rewarding?

This Week's Prayer

Pray this prayer throughout the week: *"Heavenly Father, use the history of
your people 'growing up' as a nation to teach me how to grow up as your child."*

☐ **FIRST READING** | **Deuteronomy 7–9; Psalm 9**

- How does the strong warning in Deuteronomy 8:19–20 show God's fairness?
- How does Deuteronomy 9:4–6 help explain why the conquest of Canaan was justified, and why Israel must diligently watch out for the "log in their own eye"?

☐ **SECOND READING** | **Numbers 25; Leviticus 18; Psalm 36**

- What is the connection between sexual immorality and pagan influence in Numbers 25:1–3?
- What is that same connection in Leviticus 18:1–3, 24–30? What does God promise he will do if the Israelites engage in the same immorality?

☐ **THIRD READING** | **Joshua 7; 9; Isaiah 2; Psalm 62**

- Although Achan is an Israelite, how does God deal with his sin in Joshua 7:25?
- What does Isaiah 2:3–4 indicate is God's ultimate desire for humanity?

THIS WEEK'S NOTES AND REFLECTIONS

_____

_____

_____

_____

_____

_____

_____

_____

_____

_____

_____

_____

_____

_____

_____

_____

Fast Track

IDENTIFYING SPIRITUAL ENTROPY: JUDGES 2-8

> **FIRST READING** Judges 2-4; Psalm 57
> **SECOND READING** Judges 5-6; Psalm 59
> **THIRD READING** Judges 7-8; Psalm 86

Look for. . .
- Cycles of rebellion and deliverance
- Deborah, prophetess and judge
- Gideon's daring exploits

Activity
Observe the way living things around you grow and mature: children, pets, plants, and so on. What parallels can you make between their growth—with fits and starts, beauty and bewilderment—and spiritual progress? What most frustrates you about the growth process? What is rewarding?

This Week's Prayer
Pray this prayer throughout the week: *"Heavenly Father, use the history of your people 'growing up' as a nation to teach me how to grow up as your child."*

□ **FIRST READING** | **Judges 2–4; Psalm 75**

- Judges 2:10–23 is a brief summary of the whole book.
- Repeated testing (Judges 2:22) was God's way then and now; how does the New Testament bear that out in James 1:2–4 and 1 Peter 4:12–13?
- How is the Spirit's being behind Othniel's abilities in Judges 3:10 parallel to Acts 1:8? How is the Spirit similarly active in your life these days?

□ **SECOND READING** | **Judges 5–6; Psalm 59**

- Though Deborah's leadership was rare in a patriarchal society, how do women also play an important leadership role in Exodus 15:20 and 2 Kings 22:14? What might these God-ordained exceptions be telling us about his view of women (see Acts 2:17–18 and Galatians 3:28)?
- The song in Judges 5—like the book of Psalms—fills out God's Word, which not only includes "left-brained" history but also "right-brained" poetry. Why do you think God includes both kinds of teaching in Scripture?
- Do you think Gideon's "putting out a fleece" in Judges 6:35–39 is warranted in light of Judges 6:20–22?

□ **THIRD READING** | **Judges 7–8; Psalm 86**

- What lesson might God have been trying to teach Gideon by *reducing* the troops in Judges 7:2–7?
- Even good things, when worshiped, become snares (Judges 8:27; also 2 Kings 18:4; Deuteronomy 5:8–10). What good things in your life can take on such an inflated—and harmful—role?

THIS WEEK'S NOTES AND REFLECTIONS

OTC

Fast Track

FIRST READING	Judges 11–13; Psalm 141
SECOND READING	Judges 14–16; Psalm 60
THIRD READING	Ruth; Psalm 61

Look for...

• Jephthah's rash vow
• Samson and Delilah
• "Everyone did as he saw fit" (literally, "what was right in his own eyes")
• God's faithfulness to a non-Jewish woman who joins with Israel

Activity

Observe the way living things around you grow and mature: children, pets, plants, and so on. What parallels can you make between their growth—with fits and starts, beauty and bewilderment—and spiritual progress? What most frustrates you about the growth process? What is rewarding?

This Week's Prayer

Pray this prayer throughout the week: *"Heavenly Father, use the history of your people 'growing up' as a nation to teach me how to grow up as your child."*

....

□ **FIRST READING** | **Judges 11–13; Psalm 141**

• Though the Spirit is working on Jephthah (Judges 11:29), what foolish "deal" with God did he make in Judges 11:30–31 (see Leviticus 27:1–8; Deuteronomy 12:31; 18:10; 23:21–23)?

• Have you ever experienced a spiritual "high" soon followed by great folly in your life? What principle in 1 Corinthians 10:12 can help protect you?

• Samson was a Nazirite; Numbers 6 teaches about the Nazirite vow—temporary in most cases, lifelong in Samson's (note Luke 1:15 as well).

• How does Judges 13:22 compare with 6:22–23; Genesis 32:30; and Exodus 33:20?

....

□ **SECOND READING** | **Judges 14–16; Psalm 60**

• Samson has been called "the world's weakest strong man." What aspects of his life bear that out in Judges 14:1–2, 8–9 and 16:1?

• What could happen in your life if you don't strengthen your weak areas?

• How might the Philistines see Samson's capture as vindication for their grain god, Dagon, in Judges 16:23 (see also 15:4–5)?

....

□ **THIRD READING** | **Ruth; Psalm 61**

• The Moabites, though not a part of Israel, were descendants of Lot, Abraham's nephew.

• What is a "kinsman-redeemer" (see Ruth 2:20; 3:12; 4:3–6; Leviticus 25:25, 47–49; and Deuteronomy 25:5–10)?

• Ruth's faith in God made it possible for her not only to have a place in the community of Israel but to be an ancestor of David—and eventually Jesus (Ruth 4:22; Matthew 1:5).

• How does Isaiah 56:1–8 echo God's inclusive love (the theme of this book)?

....

THIS WEEK'S NOTES AND REFLECTIONS

_____

_____

_____

_____

_____

_____

_____

OTC

Fast Track

SAMUEL: LEARNING TO LISTEN TO GOD: 1 SAMUEL 1-4; 7-8

FIRST READING	1 Samuel 1-2; Psalm 113
SECOND READING	1 Samuel 3-4; Psalm 99
THIRD READING	1 Samuel 7-8; Psalm 64

Look for. . .

- Hannah's persistent prayer pays off
- The emergence of Samuel the prophet
- The ark captured by Philistines, with disastrous results
- Israel rejects God by asking for a king

Activity

Observe the way living things around you grow and mature: children, pets, plants, and so on. What parallels can you make between their growth—with fits and starts, beauty and bewilderment—and spiritual progress? What most frustrates you about the growth process? What is rewarding?

This Week's Prayer

Pray this prayer throughout the week: *"Heavenly Father, use the history of your people 'growing up' as a nation to teach me how to grow up as your child."*

□ **FIRST READING** | **1 Samuel 1–2; Psalm 113**

- What principles of prayer can you glean from Hannah's prayer life in 1 Samuel 1:10–20, 27–28?
- First Samuel 2:5 says "seven children" though Hannah had only Samuel at that time (and eventually only six total, 1 Samuel 2:21); what does that indicate about biblical use of the number seven (see also Genesis 4:15; Psalm 12:6; Revelation 4:5)?
- How does 1 Samuel 2:26 compare with Luke 2:52?
- What is a modern-day parallel to 1 Samuel 2:17?

□ **SECOND READING** | **1 Samuel 3–4; Psalm 99**

- In what way can you cultivate attitudes similar to those expressed in 1 Samuel 3:10 and 19?
- What common parenting mistake is seen in 1 Samuel 3:13?
- How does 1 Samuel 4:1–11 illustrate that it is more important to take God's side than to try to make him take yours?

□ **THIRD READING** | **1 Samuel 7–8; Psalm 64**

- Samuel, like Eli before him, had disobedient children (1 Samuel 8:3)—a possibility even for godly parents.
- What insight does 1 Samuel 8:20 give as to why wanting a king was a rejection of God (see also 1 Samuel 8:7)?

THIS WEEK'S NOTES AND REFLECTIONS

_____

_____

_____

_____

_____

_____

_____

_____

_____

OTC

Fast Track

SAUL: WHERE IS YOUR CONFIDENCE? 1 SAMUEL 9-10; 13; 15-16; 18; 24; 28; 31

FIRST READING	1 Samuel 9-10; 13; Psalm 21
SECOND READING	1 Samuel 15-16; 18; Psalm 101
THIRD READING	1 Samuel 24; 28; 31; Psalm 54

Look for...

- Saul chosen as king
- Saul's halfhearted obedience
- God rejects Saul as king
- Saul's irrational jealousy, rage, and depression
- David spares Saul's life
- Saul consults a medium with disastrous results

Activity

Observe the way living things around you grow and mature: children, pets, plants, and so on. What parallels can you make between their growth—with fits and starts, beauty and bewilderment—and spiritual progress? What most frustrates you about the growth process? What is rewarding?

This Week's Prayer

Pray this prayer throughout the week: *"Heavenly Father, use the history of your people 'growing up' as a nation to teach me how to grow up as your child."*

☐ **FIRST READING** | **1 Samuel 9–10; 13; Psalm 21**

• Why do the superficial leadership qualifications in 1 Samuel 9:1–2 impress people even today?

• What is Saul's view of himself based on 1 Samuel 9:21 and 10:21–22?

• What "religious" words and actions cover up a disobedient heart in 1 Samuel 13:8–13?

• God is still looking for "wholehearted" followers (1 Samuel 13:14); how is your heart these days?

☐ **SECOND READING** | **1 Samuel 15–16; 18; Psalm 101**

• What parallel can you make between 1 Samuel 15:22–23 and Psalm 51:16–17?

• How do you see God's leadership qualifications from 1 Samuel 16:7 shown in his ultimate leader, the Messiah, in Isaiah 53:2–3?

• Read 1 Samuel 18:15–16. What would you tell Saul to do?

☐ **THIRD READING** | **1 Samuel 24; 28; 31; Psalm 54**

• How does 1 Samuel 24 illustrate Matthew 5:43–44; Romans 12:19–21; and 1 Peter 2:18–23?

• Saul's visit with a medium is a last-ditch effort of a desperate man; what does God say in Deuteronomy 18:10–11 and Isaiah 8:19–20 about the practice?

• What steps can you take to make sure God's potential in you isn't wasted as it was with Saul?

THIS WEEK'S NOTES AND REFLECTIONS

_____

_____

_____

_____

_____

_____

_____

_____

OTC

Fast Track

FINDING JESUS IN THE OLD TESTAMENT: ISAIAH 9; 11; 53; ZECHARIAH 12:10; MICAH 5:1–2;
EZEKIEL 37; DANIEL 7:1–14

FIRST READING	Isaiah 9; 11; Psalm 2
SECOND READING	Isaiah 53; Zechariah 12:10; Psalm 91
THIRD READING	Micah 5:1–2; Ezekiel 37; Daniel 7:1–14; Psalm 110

Look for...
- A "great light" to come in Galilee
- Child will be "Mighty God ... Prince of Peace"
- Servant will suffer and be "pierced" before reigning in power
- Ruler from Bethlehem will shepherd God's people
- Coming "Son of Man" will be worshiped and will rule the universe

Activity
Observe the way living things around you grow and mature: children,
pets, plants, and so on. What parallels can you make between their
growth—with fits and starts, beauty and bewilderment—and spiritual
progress? What most frustrates you about the growth process? What is
rewarding?

This Week's Prayer
Pray this prayer throughout the week: *"Heavenly Father, use the history of
your people 'growing up' as a nation to teach me how to grow up as your child."*

☐ FIRST READING | Isaiah 9; 11; Psalm 2

- From Galilee comes a "great light" (Isaiah 9:1–2), who is more than human (9:6–7): Messiah Jesus. How did the Pharisees miss—or reject—this verse in John 7:52?
- The Branch (Isaiah 11:1), the Root of Jesse (11:10), is none other than Jesus (Jeremiah 23:5; 33:15; Zechariah 3:8–9; 6:12–13), who will bring peace everywhere someday (Isaiah 11:6–9).

☐ SECOND READING | Isaiah 53; Zechariah 12:10; Psalm 91

- Isaiah 53 is one of the most amazing chapters in the whole Old Testament, accurately predicting Jesus' death (verses 4–8), burial (verse 9), resurrection (verses 10–11), and atonement (verses 4–6, 11–12).
- In Zechariah 12:10, God describes himself as "pierced"; when did this happen (compare John 19:33–37)?

☐ THIRD READING | Micah 5:1–2; Ezekiel 37; Daniel 7:1–14; Psalm 110

- Where will the future ruler of Israel come from according to Micah 5:2?
- The future shepherd-king David (Ezekiel 37:27) was Jesus; when will he completely fulfill this promise according to Revelation 21:1–3?
- Who but the human/divine Jesus could fulfill Daniel 7:14?

THIS WEEK'S NOTES AND REFLECTIONS

_____

_____

_____

_____

_____

_____

_____

_____

_____

_____

_____

OTC

Fast Track

DAVID: DEVELOPING A HEART FOR GOD: 1 SAMUEL 17; 2 SAMUEL 5–6; 9; 11–15; 18;
PSALMS 18; 23; 51

FIRST READING	1 Samuel 17; 2 Samuel 5–6; 9; Psalm 18
SECOND READING	2 Samuel 11–13; Psalm 51
THIRD READING	2 Samuel 14–15, 18; Psalm 23

Look for...
- Young David defeats Goliath
- David becomes king
- David's enthusiastic worship
- Mephibosheth included
- David and Bathsheba
- David's failures as a father

Activity
Often we seek God's presence to comfort us in times of trouble. Yet what
about times of relative "success"; how do we tend to respond to him then?
This week look for God's presence in the "highs" as you live day to day.
When you are in a positive experience, reflect on God's involvement with
you at that moment. How does being mindful of God make a difference?

This Week's Prayer
Pray this prayer throughout the week: *"God, teach me to enjoy seasons of
blessing in ways that bring me closer to you."*

□ **FIRST READING** | **1 Samuel 17; 2 Samuel 5–6; 9; Psalm 18**

• What past victories in your life give you the type of confidence David had in 1 Samuel 17:37?

• How was touching the ark (2 Samuel 6:6–7) a clear violation of Numbers 4:15? What is something "holy"—person or principle—that you need to treat with greater reverence?

• Enthusiastic worshipers: Take heart from David's example (2 Samuel 6:14, 21–22)!

• How is 2 Samuel 9:1 a fulfillment of David's oath in 1 Samuel 20:12–15?

□ **SECOND READING** | **2 Samuel 11–13; Psalm 51**

• Sin produces a "cover-up" (2 Samuel 11:6–13), leading to murder (11:15); but what is a biblically guaranteed outcome of every cover-up (1 Timothy 5:24)?

• Nathan's clever confrontation (2 Samuel 12:1–10) has the desired effect (12:13); though God forgives David's sin (12:13), what consequences remain (12:14)?

• Though explicit teaching in the Old Testament is rare, how does 2 Samuel 12:23 (see also Deuteronomy 32:50 and Job 19:25–27) hint at the idea of an afterlife?

• Lust—when acted on—is never like the fantasy; how does indulged-in sin finally disappoint in 2 Samuel 13:15? What lessons have you learned about the disappointing effects of sin?

□ **THIRD READING** | **2 Samuel 14–15, 18; Psalm 23**

• What is happening to David's self-confidence in 2 Samuel 15:14 and 19? (Note the title he gives Absalom.)

• How strong is parental love—even in the face of rebelliousness (see 2 Samuel 18:33)?

• Read Matthew 23:37. How is David's lament for Absalom an echo of God's anguish for his disobedient sons and daughters?

THIS WEEK'S NOTES AND REFLECTIONS

OTC

Fast Track

THE HEIGHTS AND DEPTHS OF PRAYER: PSALMS 33-35; 42; 58; 100; 103; 117; 137

FIRST READING	Psalms 42; 103; 137
SECOND READING	Psalms 33-35
THIRD READING	Psalms 58; 100; 117

Look for...
- Psalms of praise (joy)
- Psalms of lament (sadness)
- Parallel phrases that repeat or expand an idea, or sometimes show contrast
- The shortest chapter in the Bible

Activity
Often we seek God's presence to comfort us in times of trouble. Yet what about times of relative "success"; how do we tend to respond to him then? This week look for God's presence in the "highs" as you live day to day. When you are in a positive experience, reflect on God's involvement with you at that moment. How does being mindful of God make a difference?

This Week's Prayer
Pray this prayer throughout the week: *"God, teach me to enjoy seasons of blessing in ways that bring me closer to you."*

☐ **FIRST READING** | **Psalms 42; 103; 137**

• What is your reaction to the mood of the psalmist in Psalm 42?
• What are the main problems the psalmist faces in Psalm 42:9–10?
• How do the moods of Psalm 103 and 137 compare?

☐ **SECOND READING** | **Psalms 33–35**

• Should we take the account of God's creation in Psalm 33:6–9 as figures of speech or literally? Why do you think God sometimes expresses doctrine poetically not just propositionally?
• How is the image of a lion used differently in Psalm 34:10 and 35:17?
• In Psalm 34:6–7 everything has turned out right for David, yet in Psalm 35:20–25, he is in deep trouble. Are these psalms contradictory?

☐ **THIRD READING** | **Psalms 58; 100; 117**

• What is the tone of Psalm 58? How could a godly person like David express such anger?
• In Psalm 100, we offer thanks and praise because we are "owned" by God. How does his ownership of you make your heart thankful today?
• Psalm 117 is the shortest chapter of the Bible—but a wonderful burst of praise!

THIS WEEK'S NOTES AND REFLECTIONS

Fast Track

THE GREATEST PRAYERS OF ALL TIMES: PSALMS 30; 69; 74; 83; 94; 96; 119:1–112

FIRST READING	Psalms 30; 69; 96
SECOND READING	Psalm 119:1–112
THIRD READING	Psalms 74; 83; 94

Look for. . .
- Psalms that cry out for judgment against wicked people
- Psalms that thank God for intervening
- Psalms that recognize God's enthronement over all
- The longest chapter in the Bible

Activity
Often we seek God's presence to comfort us in times of trouble. Yet what about times of relative "success"; how do we tend to respond to him then? This week look for God's presence in the "highs" as you live day to day. When you are in a positive experience, reflect on God's involvement with you at that moment. How does being mindful of God make a difference?

This Week's Prayer
Pray this prayer throughout the week: *"God, teach me to enjoy seasons of blessing in ways that bring me closer to you."*

☐ **FIRST READING** | **Psalms 30; 69; 96**

- Psalm 30 is a follow-up to a complaint; as we pour out our concerns to God, it is good to thank him after the fact (see Luke 17:11–18).
- What are some of the figures of speech David uses in Psalm 69 to describe his distress? How well do these relate to your own experience?
- How naturally do the feelings in Psalm 96 come to you? What's the point of describing nonpersonal objects (verses 11–13) as if they can sing to and praise God?

☐ **SECOND READING** | **Psalm 119:1–112**

- Just as the various psalms have contrasting moods, they have contrasting lengths; this is the longest chapter in the Bible (just as Psalm 117 is the shortest).
- What's the common emphasis in all the verses of Psalm 119? What do you think is the point of this repetition?
- How can you apply verses 9 and 11 to your daily struggles with sin?
- What connection can you make between the limitations of the light shed by the lamp in verse 105 and how much "advance notice" God gives us in life? Is that light still adequate?

☐ **THIRD READING** | **Psalms 74; 83; 94**

- Why does God allow periods in our life such as are described in Psalm 74:9?
- Rather than just personal revenge, what does the psalmist have in mind as he cries out for justice in Psalm 83:17–18?
- When political realms become corrupt (Psalm 94:20–21), what ultimate comfort can we as believers take (verses 22–23)?

THIS WEEK'S NOTES AND REFLECTIONS

_____

_____

_____

_____

_____

_____

_____

Fast Track

ENTER THE ROMANCE: SONG OF SONGS

> FIRST READING   Song of Songs 1–3; Psalm 45
> SECOND READING   Song of Songs 4–5; Psalm 65
> THIRD READING   Song of Songs 6–8; Psalm 128

Look for...
- Frank expression of romantic love
- Poetic descriptions of sensuality
- "Lover and friend"
- Don't awaken love before its proper time

Activity
Did your family have any "wise sayings" that were often repeated or passed down? What are some of your favorite "quotes to live by" that don't come from the Bible? Over the coming weeks, make a collection of your own "Words of Wisdom" that have shaped your life.

This Week's Prayer
Pray this prayer throughout the week: *"God, give me wisdom from everyday life as well as enable me to learn truth from your Word."*

☐ **FIRST READING** | **Song of Songs 1–3; Psalm 45**

- Song of Songs is an unabashed celebration of marital love; how does 1:2 set the tone for what's to come?
- Song of Songs 2:7 (also 3:5; 8:4) is an admonition about not rushing sexual intimacy; is that a message you need to hear?
- "Solomon" (Song of Songs 3:7–11) may be metaphorical, the groom being "kingly" in the beloved's sight (in 1:7 he's a shepherd).

☐ **SECOND READING** | **Song of Songs 4–5; Psalm 65**

- Why should "sister" (Song of Songs 4:9) be understood as an intimate relationship, not literal sibling (compare with "friend" in 5:16)?
- The descriptions in Song of Songs 4:1–7; 5:10–16; 6:4–9 sound strange to our ears; what do you know about biblical culture that would cause listeners to consider them beautiful?

☐ **THIRD READING** | **Song of Songs 6–8; Psalm 128**

- What exclusivity is noted in Song of Songs 7:10 that is an important ingredient to successful marriages (see Genesis 2:24; Matthew 19:4–6; 1 Corinthians 7:3–5)?
- "Wall" and "door" (Song of Songs 8:9–10) may refer to opposites: guarded purity and moral laxity; what is the writer saying about those two conditions?

THIS WEEK'S NOTES AND REFLECTIONS

Fast Track

SOLOMON'S EXTREME WISDOM: 1 KINGS 1-3; PROVERBS 1; 5-7; 10-11; 24-26

FIRST READING	1 Kings 1-3; Psalm 132
SECOND READING	Proverbs 1; 5-7; Psalm 127
THIRD READING	Proverbs 10-11; 24-26; Psalm 116

Look for...
• King David's final days
• Solomon's prayer for wisdom
• Solomon's wise resolution of a dispute
• Proverbs that explore and explain practical living

Activity
Did your family have any "wise sayings" that were often repeated or passed down? What are some of your favorite "quotes to live by" that don't come from the Bible? Over the coming weeks, make a collection of your own "Words of Wisdom" that have shaped your life.

This Week's Prayer
Pray this prayer throughout the week: *"God, give me wisdom from everyday life as well as enable me to learn truth from your Word."*

☐ **FIRST READING** | **1 Kings 1–3; Psalm 132**

• How would you summarize the last days—and final instructions—of King David?
• How does 1 Kings 3:10–14 illustrate Matthew 6:33?
• What remarkable wisdom does Solomon display in 1 Kings 3:16–28?

☐ **SECOND READING** | **Proverbs 1; 5–7; Psalm 127**

• How would you explain "fear of the LORD" in light of 1 John 4:18? (See also Psalm 112, especially the contrasting "fears" in verses 1 and 7–8.)
• According to Proverbs 1:20–21, how widely available is "wisdom"?
• In addition to avoiding the act of immorality, what else should we do according to Proverbs 5:8?
• Proverbs 7 is a masterful description of the series of choices you have to take to "fall" into adultery; how many steps can you identify?

☐ **THIRD READING** | **Proverbs 10–11; 24–26; Psalm 116**

• What does Jesus say about Proverbs 24:29 in Luke 6:27–28?
• How does Jesus use Proverbs 25:7 in Luke 14:7–11?
• Do Proverbs 26:4 and 5 contradict? The key is the word "according," used with slight differences in each verse (made clear by the second phrase of each verse).
• How does Peter use Proverbs 26:11 in 2 Peter 2:22?

THIS WEEK'S NOTES AND REFLECTIONS

_____

_____

_____

_____

_____

_____

_____

_____

_____

_____

OTC

Fast Track

SOLOMON'S EXTREME FOLLY: NUMBERS 33:50–56;
DEUTERONOMY 16:21–17:20; 1 KINGS 4:20–34; 8–11

FIRST READING	Numbers 33:50–56; Deuteronomy 16:21–17:20; Psalm 115
SECOND READING	1 Kings 4:20–34; 8; Psalm 72
THIRD READING	1 Kings 9–11; Psalm 49

Look for...

• Warnings for kings not to abuse power or compromise spiritually
• Solomon's wealth and wisdom
• Solomon's prayer dedicating the temple
• Solomon's wives and wealth lead him astray

Activity

Did your family have any "wise sayings" that were often repeated or passed down? What are some of your favorite "quotes to live by" that don't come from the Bible? Over the coming weeks, make a collection of your own "Words of Wisdom" that have shaped your life.

This Week's Prayer

Pray this prayer throughout the week: *"God, give me wisdom from everyday life as well as enable me to learn truth from your Word."*

☐ **FIRST READING** | **Numbers 33:50–56; Deuteronomy 16:21–17:20; Psalm 115**

- What spiritual principle is taught in Numbers 33:51–52?
- How does Numbers 33:55–56 help explain why such extreme measures were necessary during the conquest of Canaan?
- How is the warning of Deuteronomy 17:16–20 borne out many years later in 1 Kings 11?

☐ **SECOND READING** | **1 Kings 4:20–34; 8; Psalm 72**

- How does Solomon's wisdom extend to nature—God's creation (1 Kings 4:33)?
- What New Testament insight into "wisdom" does James 3:13–18 give?
- How does the New Testament (Acts 7:47–50) agree with Solomon (1 Kings 8:27)?
- In what way is Solomon's prayer "evangelistic" (1 Kings 8:41–43; see also Deuteronomy 4:6 and Genesis 12:3)?
- How does Paul agree with 1 Kings 8:46 in Romans 3:10–18?

☐ **THIRD READING** | **1 Kings 9–11; Psalm 49**

- Recent archaeological excavations—on the so-called Solomonic gates—confirm Solomon's renovations in the three cities mentioned at the end of 1 Kings 9:15. How can this reinforce confidence in the accuracy of the Old Testament?
- How does spiritual, not just temporal, power fulfill God's intentions for Israel and make Solomon renown in 1 Kings 10:1? (Notice Jesus' allusion to this in Matthew 12:42.)
- Did Solomon's wisdom fail, or did he fail to follow wisdom in 1 Kings 11:9–10?

THIS WEEK'S NOTES AND REFLECTIONS

Fast Track

JOB: WHERE IS GOD WHEN IT HURTS? JOB 1-4; 6; 8; 11; 19; 23; 38:1-7; 40; 42

> **FIRST READING** Job 1-4; Psalm 55
>
> **SECOND READING** Job 6; 8; 11; 19; Psalm 130
>
> **THIRD READING** Job 23; 38:1-7; 40; 42; Psalm 31

Look for...
- Satan accuses Job of a "fair-weather friendship" with God
- God allows—and limits—Satan's testing of Job
- Job's friends falsely accuse Job of wrongdoing
- Job maintains his integrity and cries out to be vindicated
- God finally shows up, rebuking all but vindicating Job
- Job's fortunes are restored

Activity
Pay attention to what people do to help those who suffer. What words are used? What actions are taken? What words and actions seem to truly help? What words and actions make the problem worse?

This Week's Prayer
Pray this prayer throughout the week: *"God, show me how to help those who suffer without sounding like Job's friends."*

☐ **FIRST READING** | **Job 1-4; Psalm 55**

- Satan's accusation (Job 1:9-11) echoes through the ages: Do we love God only because of his benefits, or for who he is? How does *your* life answer that question?
- What do the limits put on Satan (Job 1:12; 2:6) tell you about God's power—and Satan's?

- What did Job's friends do right in Job 2:13? Why do you think we often feel the need to talk instead of just "be with" those in pain?
- Here's an important tip for understanding this book: In Job 42:7, God says things spoken by Job's friends are wrong; Job himself admits many of his words were wrong too (42:2–6). Therefore, this book contains lots of theological errors—*correctly recorded!* No statement of Job or especially of his friends should be assumed as good theology without corroboration elsewhere in Scripture (some examples to be "questioned": 5:12; 6:14; 7:7, 15–16).

☐ SECOND READING | Job 6; 8; 11; 19; Psalm 130

- According to Job 6:14, do real friends leave when a person has a crisis of faith?
- Notice the ironies in Job 8:4–7; Job did offer sacrifices for what his kids might have done wrong (1:4–5), but is that why they died? Job's latter days were prosperous, but for the reason Bildad suggests? Job was pure and upright (8:6), but isn't that precisely why Satan attacked him?
- What will "heal" Job, according to Zophar in Job 11:14–15?
- What is the common theme in Job 19:25–27 and the following passages: Zechariah 14:3–4; 2 Corinthians 5:1–4; 1 John 3:2; Revelation 1:7?

☐ THIRD READING | Job 23, 38:1–7; 40; 42; Psalm 31

- How does Job describe the benefits that trials can bring in Job 23:10? (James and Peter agree in James 1:2–4 and 1 Peter 1:6–7.)
- In Job's circumstances, his friends presumed his guilt; Job presumed God's anger or injustice. Was either right (Job 38:2)?
- Ultimately, a lover doesn't need answers; a lover needs the beloved (Job 42:5–6). God shows up for Job—and for all of us someday (Revelation 21:3–4).
- What is the connection between God's blessing and praying for others in Job 42:10?

THIS WEEK'S NOTES AND REFLECTIONS

Fast Track

DIVIDED KINGDOM: WHAT PUTS COMMUNITY AT RISK?
1 KINGS 12; 14-16; 2 CHRONICLES 14-16

FIRST READING	1 Kings 12; 14; Psalm 120
SECOND READING	1 Kings 15-16; Psalm 122
THIRD READING	2 Chronicles 14-16; Psalm 89

Look for...
- Golden age of Israel fades into civil war, division
- Rehoboam "powers up" over the nation
- Jeroboam sets up golden calves
- Abijah's halfhearted devotion to God
- Asa starts out well but ends in oppression
- "Eyes of the LORD range throughout the earth..."

Activity
The kings of Israel and Judah often used their power in corrupt ways. Yet they did not have to. This week, notice settings in which you are powerful—or could be. Guided by the Holy Spirit, use your power to cheer a friend, influence a child, take a stand for integrity, or encourage a coworker. Intentionally live out Proverbs 3:27, "Do not withhold good from those who deserve it, when it is in your power to act."

This Week's Prayer
Pray this prayer throughout the week: *"God, show me my power, use it for good, and protect me from pride."*

☐ **FIRST READING** | **1 Kings 12, 14; Psalm 120**

- After Solomon's death, Israel (north) and Judah (south) become two nations, never again to be a politically united people (but note Ezekiel 37:15–28).
- Age doesn't guarantee wisdom, but why is it folly for Rehoboam to reject his older counselors (1 Kings 12:8; Leviticus 19:32)?
- Compare 1 Kings 12:28 with Exodus 32:4; what political ends cause spiritual compromise (1 Kings 12:27)?
- How is pagan worship (1 Kings 14:23–24) a way of "hedging your bets" in case God doesn't come through? Why might the sexual aspects of such "worship" also hold an appeal?

☐ **SECOND READING** | **1 Kings 15–16; Psalm 122**

- The litany of bad kings climaxes with King Ahab (1 Kings 16:30–33).
- What judgment of God (Joshua 6:26) proved true in the case of Hiel in 1 Kings 16:34?
- Do you think God curses disobedience, or is disobedience its own curse? What have you seen in your own life to support your answer?

☐ **THIRD READING** | **2 Chronicles 14–16; Psalm 89**

- What do 2 Chronicles 15:16; Matthew 10:37; and Psalm 27:10 say about loyalty to God above family?
- What insight does 2 Chronicles 16:7–9 give on the sin behind Asa's treaty in 1 Kings 15:18–19?
- The beginning of 2 Chronicles 16:9 has a timeless principle; how is your heart?

THIS WEEK'S NOTES AND REFLECTIONS

_____
_____
_____
_____
_____
_____
_____
_____
_____

OTC

Fast Track

ELIJAH: HOLDING STEADY IN A ROLLER-COASTER WORLD: 1 KINGS 17–19:14

FIRST READING	1 Kings 17; Psalm 63
SECOND READING	1 Kings 18; Psalm 97
THIRD READING	1 Kings 19:1–14; Psalm 139

Look for . . .
- Elijah fed by ravens
- Flour and oil miraculously extended
- Boy raised from the dead
- Test on Mount Carmel
- Elijah depressed

Activity
The kings of Israel and Judah often used their power in corrupt ways. Yet they did not have to. This week, notice settings in which you are powerful—or could be. Guided by the Holy Spirit, use your power to cheer a friend, influence a child, take a stand for integrity, or encourage a coworker. Intentionally live out Proverbs 3:27, "Do not withhold good from those who deserve it, when it is in your power to act."

This Week's Prayer
Pray this prayer throughout the week: *"God, show me my power, use it for good, and protect me from pride."*

☐ **FIRST READING** | **1 Kings 17; Psalm 63**

- What does James 5:17–18 say about 1 Kings 17:1?
- How does God's mercy to a non-Jew in 1 Kings 17:9–16 show his intent to reach out to Gentiles and illustrate his gracious choice of unworthy sinners? (Note also Jesus' comments in Luke 4:25–26.)
- What similarities do you see between 1 Kings 17:21 and Acts 20:9–12?

☐ **SECOND READING** | **1 Kings 18; Psalm 97**

- Elijah's sarcasm is biting, but revealing (1 Kings 18:27).
- How does the story in 1 Kings 18:28–29 demonstrate that "sincerity" in religion is not enough? How do Paul's words in Romans 10:2 shed light on what else is needed?
- How is Baal, the god of water, further humiliated by God's power in 1 Kings 18:33–35, 38?

☐ **THIRD READING** | **1 Kings 19:1–14; Psalm 139**

- What surprising mood follows Elijah's great ministry triumph in 1 Kings 19:4–5? Have you ever experienced this? (If so, you're in good company!)
- What practical help did God send in 1 Kings 19:5–9?

THIS WEEK'S NOTES AND REFLECTIONS

_____

_____

_____

_____

_____

_____

_____

_____

_____

_____

_____

_____

OTC

Fast Track

ELISHA: RECEIVING A SPIRITUAL LEGACY: 1 KINGS 19:15-21; 2 KINGS 2-6

FIRST READING	1 Kings 19:15-21; 2 Kings 2; Psalm 84
SECOND READING	2 Kings 3-4; Psalm 145
THIRD READING	2 Kings 5-6; Psalm 144

Look for. . .
- Elijah told by God to appoint his successor
- Elijah taken up to heaven
- Elisha continues doing miracles
- Invisible spiritual armies seen by Elisha and his servant

Activity
How many of your friends know their family history? How much of yours do you know? How does knowing—or not knowing—the legacy of your family affect you? What defining moments in your own life would you like future generations to remember?

This Week's Prayer
Pray this prayer throughout the week: *"God, help me take note of and pass on my life's lessons."*

☐ **FIRST READING** | **1 Kings 19:15–21; 2 Kings 2; Psalm 84**

- What important "legacy" assignment does God give Elijah in 1 Kings 19:16?
- What resolve do you see in Elisha's actions in 1 Kings 19:21?
- What question, similar to Elijah's in 2 Kings 2:9, should leaders in our day ask of those they lead?
- Elijah's miraculous end (2 Kings 2:11) foreshadows what miraculous events in the messianic era (Malachi 4:5–6; Luke 9:28–33; possibly Revelation 11:3–12)?

☐ **SECOND READING** | **2 Kings 3–4; Psalm 145**

- Is "sincere" idolatry justified (2 Kings 3:27)?
- God's miracles sometimes conform to humanly imposed limits; how big are the "containers" you're giving him to fill (2 Kings 4:3–6; John 2:6–11)?
- What parallels do you see in 2 Kings 4:42–44 and John 6:5–14?

☐ **THIRD READING** | **2 Kings 5–6; Psalm 144**

- Disease is not a sign of God's disfavor (2 Kings 5:1), yet God sometimes does heal this side of heaven (2 Kings 5:13–14); in the end, all will be healed (Revelation 22:1–3).
- Naaman associates God with the land of Israel (2 Kings 5:17); what would Jesus say (John 4:19–24)?
- How serious is lying to God (2 Kings 5:23–27; Acts 5:1–11)?
- How are spiritual realities in some ways more real than physical (2 Kings 6:15–17; 2 Corinthians 4:16–18)?

THIS WEEK'S NOTES AND REFLECTIONS

_____

_____

_____

_____

_____

_____

_____

_____

_____

Fast Track

AMOS: HOW GOD MEASURES A LIFE: THE BOOK OF AMOS

FIRST READING	Amos 1–3; Psalm 82
SECOND READING	Amos 4–6; Psalm 140
THIRD READING	Amos 7–9; Psalm 146

Look for...
• Judgment starts with pagan nations but ends up with Israel
• The needy sold "for a pair of sandals"
• God welcomes justice, not religious feasts
• A "plumb line" given by God to measure spiritual uprightness

Activity
Generally we prefer encouraging words to corrective ones. But both are necessary. During the coming weeks, notice all the messages around you designed to warn or rebuke: at home, the office, school, newspapers, TV, Internet, and so on. Which ones seem effective? Which don't get heard? What makes you more receptive—or defensive?

This Week's Prayer
Pray this prayer throughout the week: *"God, open me up to correction— whenever needed, from whomever you send."*

☐ **FIRST READING** | **Amos 1–3; Psalm 82**

- All the nations in Amos 1 surround Israel; how might this be a set up for the punch line in Amos 2:4 and 6?
- What economic and moral failures do you see in Amos 2:6–8?
- How does Amos's rhetorical question about human interactions in Amos 3:3 echo truth about human/divine interaction as well?

☐ **SECOND READING** | **Amos 4–6; Psalm 140**

- How does Matthew 8:10–12 illustrate Amos 5:18?
- How does the principle in 1 Corinthians 10:12 apply to Amos 6:1?
- What's the point of comparing God to a builder with a plumb line (Amos 7:7–8)? What is that plumb line today?

☐ **THIRD READING** | **Amos 7–9; Psalm 146**

- People who reject God sometimes get their wish—namely, his absence (Amos 8:11–12).
- How did the early church understand the promise of Amos 9:11–12 (see Acts 15:13–19)?

THIS WEEK'S NOTES AND REFLECTIONS

Fast Track

ISAIAH: PURSUING SPIRITUAL AUTHENTICITY: ISAIAH 2–6; 40; 43; 56; 66

FIRST READING	Isaiah 2–4; Psalm 93
SECOND READING	Isaiah 5–6; 40; Psalm 104
THIRD READING	Isaiah 43; 56; 66; Psalm 85

Look for...
- Swords into plowshares, spears into pruning hooks
- Song for the vineyard
- Isaiah's vision of God, sinful lips cleansed
- Comfort to come
- God the Savior will reign

Activity
Generally we prefer encouraging words to corrective ones. But both are necessary. During the coming weeks, notice all the messages around you designed to warn or rebuke: at home, the office, school, newspapers, TV, Internet, and so on. Which ones seem effective? Which don't get heard? What makes you more receptive—or defensive?

This Week's Prayer
Pray this prayer throughout the week: *"God, open me up to correction—whenever needed, from whomever you send."*

☐ **FIRST READING** | Isaiah 2–4; Psalm 93

- What parallels can you make to Judah's sins in Isaiah 2:6–8 and people in our day?
- "Children" (Isaiah 3:4) is meant literally (2 Kings 21:1), but how is it also symbolic (2 Kings 23:36–37; 24:8–9, 18–19)?
- The "Branch" (Isaiah 4:2; 11:1–5) is Messiah. The mission described here began with Jesus' first coming; when will it culminate (Hebrews 9:28; 2 Thessalonians 1:6–10)?

☐ **SECOND READING** | Isaiah 5–6; 40; Psalm 104

- Despite bad political news (Isaiah 6:1; 2 Chronicles 26), Isaiah saw God enthroned in power. Is that still true when hard news reaches us today?
- How did Jesus use Isaiah 6:9–10 in Matthew 13:13–15?
- John the Baptist saw himself fulfilling Isaiah 40:3 (Mark 1:2–4).
- Can we still count on the promise of Isaiah 40:8 today (Isaiah 55:11; Jeremiah 23:29; Matthew 24:35; 1 Peter 1:24–25)?

☐ **THIRD READING** | Isaiah 43, 56, 66; Psalm 85

- You, too, are redeemed (Isaiah 43:1) and precious to him (43:4). Do you believe this? What difference will it make today?
- God's "I am he" (Isaiah 41:4; 43:10, 13, 25; 46:4; 48:12) is repeated by Jesus (John 8:56–58; 13:19; 18:6; Mark 13:6); what mere man would say that?
- Our God loves to find lost sheep (Isaiah 56:8)!
- How does Jesus use Isaiah 66:1 in Matthew 5:34–35?

THIS WEEK'S NOTES AND REFLECTIONS

_____

_____

_____

_____

_____

_____

_____

_____

_____

_____

OTC

Fast Track

HEZEKIAH: RADICAL TRUST: 2 CHRONICLES 30-32; ISAIAH 7-8; 36-39

FIRST READING	2 Chronicles 30-32; Psalm 118
SECOND READING	Isaiah 7-8; Psalm 102
THIRD READING	Isaiah 36-39; Psalm 121

Look for...

• Promise of Immanuel to Ahaz

• Hezekiah leads a revival

• Assyria threatens Jerusalem

• Hezekiah "spreads out the letter" before the Lord

• Sennacherib withdraws

Activity

Generally we prefer encouraging words to corrective ones. But both are necessary. During the coming weeks, notice all the messages around you designed to warn or rebuke: at home, the office, school, newspapers, TV, Internet, and so on. Which ones seem effective? Which don't get heard? What makes you more receptive—or defensive?

This Week's Prayer

Pray this prayer throughout the week: *"God, open me up to correction— whenever needed, from whomever you send."*

☐ **FIRST READING** | **2 Chronicles 30–32; Psalm 118**

- Hezekiah's attempt at unity (2 Chronicles 30:1), some 250 years after the national split, is a testimony to the depth of his "revival."
- Doesn't every prayer reach heaven (2 Chronicles 30:27)? Yes, in the sense that our omniscient God knows everything; but what else about prayer is taught in 1 Peter 3:7; 1 John 3:22; and Matthew 6:5–8?
- What was the sign of 2 Chronicles 32:24? (Read Isaiah 38:1–8.)

☐ **SECOND READING** | **Isaiah 7–8; Psalm 102**

- What is the timeless truth taught in Isaiah 7:9?
- Immanuel, "God with us" (Isaiah 7:14; 8:8), first signified a temporary deliverance from Rezin and Aram (Isaiah 7:16); in Immanuel Jesus (Matthew 1:23) we have a permanent deliverance from sin.
- Desperate people turn to the occult (Isaiah 8:19–22) rather than Scripture (8:20). Why is that still a temptation in our day?

☐ **THIRD READING** | **Isaiah 36–39; Psalm 121**

- Isaiah 36–39 records historical events, parallel to 2 Kings 18–20.
- How are Hezekiah's actions and prayer in Isaiah 37:14–20 a great example for us?
- Hezekiah's pride (Isaiah 39:2) led to judgment (39:6–7); his reaction (39:8) may mean that he was relieved or that he thought it appropriate.

THIS WEEK'S NOTES AND REFLECTIONS

OTC

Fast Track

MICAH: DOING JUSTICE: ISAIAH 1; MICAH

FIRST READING	Isaiah 1; Micah 1; Psalm 98
SECOND READING	Micah 2–4; Psalm 107
THIRD READING	Micah 5–7; Psalm 109

Look for...
- God rejects offerings from disobedient followers
- Micah rails against people who prefer comfort and drunkenness
- What does God really want? Justice, kindness, and humility with him

Activity
All of the prophets received a call from God to do their ministry. God was specific, giving them their message and empowering them to speak. Today, we who follow Christ have the same Holy Spirit. He may not give us a prophetic message, but he does lead us and guide us into acts of service. What are some assignments God has given you these days? They may be ministry, family, personal, or career related. Can you name them? How are you doing at fulfilling them?

This Week's Prayer
Pray this prayer throughout the week: *"God, make my assignments from you clear, my heart surrendered. and my obedience complete."*

☐ FIRST READING | Isaiah 1; Micah 1; Psalm 98

- Judah was very "religious," so why is God angry (Isaiah 1:11–17)?
- God's offer in Isaiah 1:18 is valid for all times—for you! How do forgiven people live according to verse 19?
- Micah uses several wordplays in Micah 1. Check margin notes in your Bible—the city names in Hebrew sound like the proclaimed judgments.

☐ SECOND READING | Micah 2–4; Psalm 107

- How are the leaders in Micah 3:9–12 like those in Matthew 7:21–23?
- The peace of Micah 4:3 (inscribed at the United Nations) will only come when God rules (verses 2, 5). Does that mean we shouldn't work for peace in the meantime (see Matthew 5:9)?

☐ THIRD READING | Micah 5–7; Psalm 109

- What amazing prophecy is found in Micah 5:2 (see Matthew 2:6)?
- Micah 6:8 is a great summary of all the Prophets. What parts of that message are especially appropriate today?
- What parallels do you observe between Micah 6:13–16 and Deuteronomy 28:38–42, 45–52?
- How does Jesus use Micah 7:6 in Matthew 10:34–36?
- What traits of God in Micah 7:18–20 do you need right now?

THIS WEEK'S NOTES AND REFLECTIONS

_____

_____

_____

_____

_____

_____

_____

_____

_____

_____

otc

Fast Track

JEREMIAH: WHEN GOD GIVES A HARD ASSIGNMENT:
JEREMIAH 1-2; 18-20; 23; 31:31-34; 37-38; LAMENTATIONS 3:22-33

FIRST READING	Jeremiah 1-2; 18; Psalm 143
SECOND READING	Jeremiah 19-20; 23; Psalm 44
THIRD READING	Jeremiah 31:31-34; 37-38; Lamentations 3:22-33; Psalm 126

Look for. . .

• A youthful Jeremiah called into God's service

• Promises of rescue but a life of difficulty

• The "weeping prophet" despairs of his life

• A new covenant to come

• God's compassion is new every morning, his faithfulness great

Activity

All of the prophets received a call from God to do their ministry. God was specific, giving them their message and empowering them to speak. Today, we who follow Christ have the same Holy Spirit. He may not give us a prophetic message, but he does lead us and guide us into acts of service. What are some assignments God has given you these days? They may be ministry, family, personal, or career related. Can you name them? How are you doing at fulfilling them?

This Week's Prayer

Pray this prayer throughout the week: *"God, make my assignments from you clear, my heart surrendered, and my obedience complete."*

☐ **FIRST READING** | Jeremiah 1–2; 18; Psalm 143

- How does Jeremiah 1:6–7 compare with 1 Timothy 4:12?
- The twofold sin of Israel was to abandon God and then try to meet their spiritual thirst on their own (Jeremiah 2:13); God didn't mind them being thirsty but knew false religion never satisfies. What "cisterns" are you digging?
- How is Jeremiah 2:25 the cry of every addict?
- Clay needs to be soft in order to be reshaped; what kind of clay is Judah according to Jeremiah 18:11–15? What kind of clay are you?

☐ **SECOND READING** | Jeremiah 19–20, 23; Psalm 44

- How hard to you think it was to deliver the message of Jeremiah 19:10–11?
- What do you learn about Jeremiah through his prayer in 20:7–18?
- In what ways does Jesus fulfill the promise of Jeremiah 23:5–6?
- What kind of dreams and prophecies *aren't* from God according to Jeremiah 23:25–40 (see also Deuteronomy 13:1–4; Lamentations 2:14; and Colossians 2:18)?

☐ **THIRD READING** | Jeremiah 31:31–34; 37–38; Lamentations 3:22–33; Psalm 126

- The "new covenant" (or "testament") of Jeremiah 31:31–34 was inaugurated by Jesus (Hebrews 8:8–12; 10:16–17); how much of it has happened for you?
- From one pit (Jeremiah 37:16) to another (38:6), things go from bad to worse, but Jeremiah stays true to God and his Word. Will you do the same?
- God's "new morning mercies" (Lamentations 3:22–23) are all the more remarkable, coming as they do to Jeremiah—and us—in the midst of great woes. What "new mercies" do you need from him today?

THIS WEEK'S NOTES AND REFLECTIONS

_____

_____

_____

_____

_____

_____

_____

OTC

Fast Track

THE LIFE-GIVING POWER OF HOPE: 2 KINGS 25; JEREMIAH 29:1-23; DANIEL 9:1-19;
EZRA 1:1-8; NEHEMIAH 1-2; MALACHI 4; PSALMS 78-79; HEBREWS 11

FIRST READING	2 Kings 25; Jeremiah 29:1-23; Daniel 9:1-19; Psalm 147
SECOND READING	Ezra 1:1-8; Nehemiah 1-2; Malachi 4; Psalm 148
THIRD READING	Psalms 78-79; Hebrews 11

Look for. . .
- Israel's history ends in captivity, then restoration to the land
- A prayer of repentance
- Israel rebuilds the temple and Jerusalem's walls
- Elijah to come before "day of the LORD"
- Summary of Israel's history: learning to live by faith with hope

Activity
With this week's reading, you've completed the Old Testament Challenge. Congratulations! From the beginning of creation to Israel's return from captivity, you've seen God at work building his "new community." Just as ancient Israel was on a journey with God, you've been on a journey. What have been the highlights? What principles from God's Word do you want to keep in focus as a reminder of what you've learned?

This Week's Prayer
Pray this prayer: *"God, long ago against impossible odds you built a kingdom; keep building it now through me."*

☐ **FIRST READING** | **2 Kings 25; Jeremiah 29:1–23; Daniel 9:1–19; Psalm 147**

- How does 2 Kings 25:4–12 contrast with the splendor that had existed in Solomon's time?
- How hard do you think it would have been to follow Jeremiah's advice given to the exiles in Jeremiah 29?
- What general principles about confessing our sins can you get from Daniel 9:4–19?

☐ **SECOND READING** | **Ezra 1:1–8; Nehemiah 1–2; Malachi 4; Psalm 148**

- Against all odds, in Ezra 1:1 what miracle happens in Cyrus's heart? (Note that Cyrus was a pagan king.)
- What principles of confession do you see in Nehemiah 1:5–11?
- How long do you suppose it took to see an answer to the prayer in Nehemiah 2:4–5?
- The last words in the Old Testament (Malachi 4:5–6) are a promise of a messenger but threats of a curse; how is this an apt summary of the history of God's people?

☐ **THIRD READING** | **Psalms 78–79; Hebrews 11**

- What highlights from Israel's history are most memorable for you in Psalms 78–79?
- In conclusion, how does Hebrews 11 summarize the main message of the Old Testament?

THIS WEEK'S NOTES AND REFLECTIONS

_____

_____

_____

_____

_____

_____

_____

_____

_____

_____

_____

_____

İNDEX ⊙F PSALMS

Read in the Fast-Track Reading Plan

We attempted to link various psalms either to historical texts that support them or to thematic passages that parallel them. Thus, they are read out of order. Here is a list of the psalms read and which week.

Willow Creek Association
Vision, Training, Resources for Prevailing Churches

This resource was created to serve you and to help you build a local church that prevails. It is just one of many ministry tools that are part of the Willow Creek Resources® line, published by the Willow Creek Association together with Zondervan.

The Willow Creek Association (WCA) was created in 1992 to serve a rapidly growing number of churches from across the denominational spectrum that are committed to helping unchurched people become fully devoted followers of Christ. Membership in the WCA now numbers over 10,000 Member Churches worldwide from more than ninety denominations.

The Willow Creek Association links like-minded Christian leaders with each other and with strategic vision, training, and resources in order to help them build prevailing churches designed to reach their redemptive potential. Here are some of the ways the WCA does that.

- **Prevailing Church Conference**—an annual two-and-a-half day event, held at Willow Creek Community Church in South Barrington, Illinois, to help pioneering church leaders raise up a volunteer core while discovering new and innovative ways to build prevailing churches that reach unchurched people.

- **Leadership Summit**—a once-a-year, two-and-a-half-day conference to envision and equip Christians with leadership gifts and responsibilities. Presented live at Willow Creek as well as via satellite broadcast to over sixty locations across North America, this event is designed to increase the leadership effectiveness of pastors, ministry staff, volunteer church leaders, and Christians in the marketplace.

- **Ministry-Specific Conferences**—throughout each year the WCA hosts a variety of conferences and training events—both at Willow Creek's main campus and offsite, across the U.S. and around the world—targeting church leaders in ministry-specific areas such as: evangelism, the arts, children, students, small groups, preaching and teaching, spiritual formation, spiritual gifts, raising up resources, etc.

- **Willow Creek Resources®**—to provide churches with trusted and field-tested ministry resources in such areas as leadership, evangelism, spiritual formation, spiritual gifts, small groups, stewardship, student ministry, children's ministry, the use of the arts—drama, media, contemporary music—and more. For additional information about Willow Creek Resources® call the Customer Service Center at 800-570-9812. Outside the U.S. call 847-765-0070.

- *WillowNet*—the WCA's Internet resource service, which provides access to hundreds of transcripts of Willow Creek messages, drama scripts, songs, videos, and multimedia tools. The system allows users to sort through these elements and download them for a fee. Visit us online at www.willowcreek.com.

- *WCA News*—a quarterly publication to inform you of the latest trends, resources, and information on WCA events from around the world.

- *Defining Moments*—a monthly audio journal for church leaders featuring Bill Hybels and other Christian leaders discussing probing issues to help you discover biblical principles and transferable strategies to maximize your church's redemptive potential.

- *The Exchange*—our online classified ads service to assist churches in recruiting key staff for ministry positions.

- **Member Benefits**—includes substantial discounts to WCA training events, a 20 percent discount on all Willow Creek Resources®, access to a Members-Only section on WillowNet, monthly communications, and more. Member Churches also receive special discounts and premier services through WCA's growing number of ministry partners—Select Service Providers.

For specific information about WCA membership, upcoming conferences, and other ministry services contact:

Willow Creek Association
P.O. Box 3188, Barrington, IL 60011-3188
Phone: 847-570-9812
Fax: 847-765-5046
www.willowcreek.com